Ya Gotta
LAUGH

BARBARA ALLDRITT

Tellwell Talent
www.tellwell.ca

ISBN
978-0-2288-5449-4 (Hardcover)
978-0-2288-5448-7 (Paperback)
978-0-2288-5450-0 (eBook)

CONTENTS

ACKNOWLEDGEMENTS

I would like to express my special thanks to my husband Michael. As my sight deteriorated, I recognised that I couldn't complete the work required to publish the book. He took on the mantle of continuing the work of helping me over the last hurdle of the final edits with the publisher/editor and the marketing. You have this book because of him.

Secondly I would like to thank those who contacted me to tell me their stories that are now written for your enjoyment.

And to friends Megan and Erin for assisting me by proofing and reading back to me my initial manuscript.

WISDOM AND ILLNESS

Beauty is truth, truth beauty—that is all
Ye know on earth, and all ye need to know.

Ode on a Grecian Urn by John Keats, 1819

I know both women and men who believe they are "not quite good enough," although the women predominate. For years I was one of these women. My psychologists called the basic problem low self-esteem. Those who live with this self-perception do their best to hide it, often very successfully. Exploring where this perspective comes from, and how to live fully despite its presence, keeps thousands of therapists in work. It also gives pharmaceutical companies outrageous profits from antidepressant drugs.

A therapist in a television interview I saw recently said that poor self-esteem usually creates workaholism. As a former workaholic, I relate to this. I graduated as the top student at my university, not because of my IQ, but because of a talent for writing and my habit of working harder and longer than others I knew. Why did I do it? I didn't ask myself this question at the time. I just did what I felt I had to do, and what got me respect and good grades from my professors.

The workaholic habits eventually took their toll on my health, however. I was diagnosed with the chronic illness called multiple sclerosis (MS) while I was at university. I was finishing a master's thesis while working on the research I expected to use for a doctoral degree. Within two years I found myself at the bottom of the social status ladder, a sick woman in a wheelchair. But it was almost as though physical illness brought a magic therapy that had eluded me for years. Soon after my diagnosis, the psychological issues that had plagued me for most of my adult life just melted away.

Accepting my new reality included a decision that there was much I could learn about myself through illness. I also started to see the qualities I had once exhibited all around me, including in places that surprised me. I saw the body language of poor self-esteem in several smart, well-educated men I know, including a PhD psychologist friend and a doctor with more certificates of achievement on his wall than anyone I've ever worked with.

Reflecting on my new health circumstances, I realized there are many different kinds of ability. The physical abilities I'd lost are the ones most of us take for granted while we have them. Getting up two stairs was never something I had to plan for before. Now, recovering my lost physical abilities consumes my time in ways I hope are positive. Losing something often highlights what is left, and I found new reserves of patience and humour. Housework and cooking became tasks for which I planned and managed other people's time rather than doing them myself. I have to admit I don't miss washing the kitchen floor. Another change I appreciate is having time for creative rather than just academic writing. It helped me accept I could now only walk in water.

My new writing focus reminds me of a conversation I had with my favourite teacher on the last day of high school. She asked me what I planned to do next.

"I'm not sure," I said, "but I plan to live enough to be able to write a book about my life."

"I'm sure you will," was her confident, smiling reply.

I had no idea that "living enough" would include disability, but, paradoxically, that is what has given me the time, confidence and subject matter to pursue my passion for creative writing.

In the electronic age we live in, this means spending a lot of time with my computer. I'd always been somewhat inept when it came to understanding the operation of anything technical like my car, my electrical appliances or my camera. This never concerned me because if anything ever went wrong, I just called the relevant repair person. Then along came the computer. I handwrote all my assignments at the beginning of university but soon learned how to use the campus mainframe computer terminals. Maybe because of my frequent all night writing sessions, my husband Michael decided to buy our own personal computer while it was still relatively uncommon to have one at home.

At first this worked well for both of us. I wrote at home and managed to get some sleep even when a deadline kept me at the computer most of the night. I don't remember anything ever going wrong with that first computer's operating system, either. I mostly used a word processing program, but I also used simple database, spreadsheet and graphic design programs. Learning the program commands was fairly straightforward, but maybe that's just nostalgia.

That first computer was slow, but it didn't matter. Now, personal computers have become very fast and powerful, and many of them operate on the system Bill Gates and his unidimensional computer geeks created. As this was the only operating system around, things started to change for the worse for me. Maybe it was my imagination, but it seemed like the operating system began intruding into my life and computing activities more. I now use my computer only for writing, keeping track of my finances and email. But as my needs simplified, the computers became much more complex. Maybe I felt the effect of this change more strongly because Michael became my resident computer support person. As they say in his hometown in England, Michael is not a man to "suffer fools gladly."

Rather than simplifying my life, the computing "improvements" resulted in my feeling a little inadequate, something I hadn't experienced in some time. One day my computer shortcomings were highlighted in a particularly embarrassing way. It was one of those urgent problems that took hours of my time and numerous phone calls to resolve, without success. When Michael came home, he saw the solution right away and reminded me that he had fixed the same problem for me a few weeks before. He thought I should have remembered, and he told me so.

But the next day I regained my self-respect. I saw that my range of knowledge extended well beyond the computer operating minutiae that had been frustrating me. I had lunch with two of the smart young computer geeks I'd called on the telephone for help to understand my problem. They could easily fix most computer problems, but our lunchtime conversation revealed that neither of them knew some facts that seemed rather basic to me. They were surprised to learn that rubber comes from a tree, that it is a natural thing, and that there are many indigenous people in the rainforests of South America who live by tapping rubber trees for their sap. My young friends did, of course, know the thousands of products made of rubber, from car tires to condoms and the soles of their shoes. I thought, though, that their understanding of the difference between natural and synthetic versions of rubber was more than a little hazy, and they seemed to think this difference had no real significance. I guess in their world it didn't.

Did those twenty-somethings feel embarrassed or inadequate because of their narrow breadth of knowledge of the world? I wondered. I'm sure they didn't. But this juxtaposition of my knowledge and interests with theirs got me reflecting on who I was and what was really important to me. I'd had to leave the world of work and keeping up not because I wanted to, but because my health forced me to. But now I'm happy with what illness has taught me and the way it has changed me.

The most important lesson, or at least the one I see affecting my response to the world most often, comes from a deep understanding that there is nothing to fear in death. While my health problems were slowly but inexorably changing every aspect of my activities and abilities, I began to wonder if I would die young because of complications caused by the MS. This was my aunt's fate.

I was just over forty when I began to wonder if the final scenes of my mortality—my death—might be closer than I had always assumed. Facing this through my intellectual bent, I decided I should read how others thought about death. My solution was to read accounts of near-death experiences. And having been a world traveller with an interest in other cultures, I also decided it was time to read *The Tibetan Book of Living and Dying.*

Both sources told me, in different ways, that there was no need to fear the transition between life and death. They told me my spirit was the bridge between the two states, and that the only thing I had to fear was fear itself. Other readings told me that the two states of life and death are in essence the same. Understanding this seeming paradox took some time, but I eventually "got it." For me it has to do with knowing that as a human I am eternal spirit first, and that the overarching importance our culture gives to the body and the mind is misplaced. I later read that those people who encounter death early in life are, in fact, fortunate because this experience deepens their appreciation for every moment in life.

That didn't mean I never felt overwhelmed by the challenges I faced. I did. I once went so far as to tell Michael that I had a plan for how to end my life if I ever felt I couldn't bear to live anymore. I was deeply touched, and somewhat surprised, when his response was to put his arms around me and tell me that he wanted to be with me if that time ever came. No denial, no evading the issue, no tears—just a deep acceptance of the validity of my right to choose when and how to die if this was what I wanted to do.

Reading old diaries reinforces what chronic illness has taught me. The diaries are filled with pain—always the same pain that flowed from a deep sense of inadequacy. I feel so light without it now, almost intoxicated with the joy of life. I'm no longer a workaholic. I accomplish a lot but not from a search for approval and acceptance. I no longer fret about a relative imperfection in the shape of my legs or the moles on my face, my hair colour or any other aspect of my appearance.

My body still has limitations, but these have led me to become stronger and more beautiful in my spiritual being. My most important challenge is to always stay in the moment and to live *in* my body rather than in some more interesting or less painful place outside of it. My spirit tells me that facing my health challenges rather than shrinking from them will take me wherever I need to go. They'll teach me whatever I'm here to learn in this life as long as I stay open to the lessons.

COMPANY AND CHANGE

May you have a strong foundation.

"Forever Young" by Bob Dylan

'm sure there's a country and western song based on the old saying "misery loves company." That was how I felt when I learned I had a debilitating and, according to my doctors, incurable chronic illness. I thought meeting others who were facing similar challenges would help me deal with my new reality. Finding company was easy. This is the rationale behind the proliferation of self-help groups for people facing everything from unwelcome new facts about health to changes in marital or work status. I soon found, though, that I needed a certain kind of company, otherwise it just created more misery.

Since my health problems had been labelled multiple sclerosis, I called the organization that specialized in working with this illness. I spoke with a counsellor named Sandra who told me that a group for the newly diagnosed would probably be the most suitable for me. Although I didn't expect to find someone who shared my interests there, it turned out that Sandra had a personal interest in what is now called alternative medicine, as I did. In part to meet Sandra, I decided to go to the next meeting, even though it was a half-hour drive from where I lived.

Entering the newly diagnosed self-help group meeting room, I joined a half dozen people sitting in a circle. Unfortunately, though, I found more misery than company. The first woman to speak described the horror she'd felt with her recent first experience of bowel incontinence. *How does one respond to a story like that?* I wondered. I had no ideas, and frankly would rather not have heard about the ordeal. It seemed others felt the same way as an awkward silence ensued. Sandra smiled stiffly and asked if anyone else wanted to share. An intense, drawn-faced man in his thirties spoke of a new drug study he'd heard was about to start in our city. He stated his intention to offer himself as a subject and promised to bring more information to the next meeting for others. I stayed the scheduled two hours of the meeting, sharing my story of numbness and disabling fatigue when asked.

As I drove home from the meeting, I reflected on why it was called a self-help group. I felt worse than when I arrived. Was the idea that sharing stressful experiences was helpful to the sharer? Was my role as a listener that of unpaid psychologist? Pooling information to allow one to help oneself was probably part of the rationale, but the only idea I heard involved offering myself as a subject in a drug study. This didn't appeal to me as I felt I'd have to give away control of my body. Besides, I'd grown up inured with the idea that drugs, legal or illegal, were to be avoided as much as possible. I felt sure I must have other options, so I decided to talk to Sandra again.

Sandra told me that the group I joined was the best she could suggest. Almost as an afterthought, she said I could always start my own group to focus on my particular interests. I decided to give it a try, and Sandra helped me place an ad in the next newsletter stating my desire to meet others who believed in taking charge of their own health through diet, stress reduction and other "alternative" strategies.

I received my first response a few weeks later from a woman who introduced herself on the phone as Liz. She told me she had just arrived home from a bike ride with her daughter, and that she didn't have much time to talk as a friend was coming to pick her up for their regular Thursday afternoon golf game. Two years ago she had needed a wheelchair, she told me. However, by regularly using a simple traditional Chinese medicine technique called moxibustion, which involves burning moxa made of ground mugwort on or near the body's meridians and acupuncture points, she was still restricted but very functional. I took her phone number and smiled to myself. *This is more like it*, I thought. *These are the kinds of self-help stories I'm interested in. Forget bowel incontinence.*

I got about a dozen more calls over the next few days, but Liz remained the star of the budding group. I organized a meeting which we held in Liz's dining room, as her home was the most central for everyone. We decided to hold meetings once a month, and I found a room provided free to community groups in a shopping centre. I published our meeting schedule and found that the meetings generated strong interest and attendance over the next few months.

We became known as the place to be to meet people like Liz and others who had recovered their health, and to learn from experts about holistic approaches to our bodies and their many functions. It didn't take long to figure out that the group was a good vehicle for getting the attention of well-known writers and researchers. One speaker even flew a thousand miles at his own expense to meet with us. The group also developed a high profile among persons with MS.

Meanwhile, Liz had a steady stream of people passing through her house to learn how to use the moxibustion technique. I tried it on myself for a time, but it had no effect on my declining energy level, and it affected my balance negatively. However, I did meet others for whom moxibustion had been positive as it had been for Liz. I decided to be encouraged by the fact that there were things that could improve one's health even after a diagnosis of MS. I hadn't found the right treatment for myself yet, but there were many others still to try.

Liz was convinced the MS Society should take on her role as teacher and mentor of the moxibustion technique. She started a petition to this effect and had no trouble getting signatures from the people she taught and from those who attended our self-help group meetings. Her petition had close to one hundred signatures when she mailed it to the executive director of the society. Her accompanying letter stated that the petition showed the interest in moxibustion and other alternative medical techniques among its members and that the society needed to do more to support these interests.

The executive director and a provincial board member called to say they'd like to attend our next meeting. There they gave us the standard lines about what the society does and how wonderful it is. None of us were very impressed by the presentation, and I left the meeting feeling skeptical about the possibility of change within the society. Liz agreed but felt we might have more success if we volunteered as directors for the board. We convinced enough others to join us, and a few months later found ourselves with majority control on the local chapter board.

The business meetings were dull, but the enthusiasm and energy of the new members shone clearly. After some initial reserve, the board member who had attended our meeting accepted the validity of our views. He used his experience to help us develop a clearly worded motion to direct the society to collect and disseminate information on alternative medical approaches to MS.

I began writing articles on holistic approaches to health for the society's newsletter. Although there was a little tension with the editors because I was writing about treatments that were different to those of conventional medicine, my articles became very popular. To my great surprise, about six months after we joined the board the executive director suggested a provincial conference to address the holistic health interests of the membership.

I agreed to chair the planning process. We solicited the input of a new institute to advance alternative medical information among conventional practitioners. Although there were a few kinks in the lines of communication and decision-making, the planning committee soon had high profile speakers from across North America for the day-and-a-half-long conference. The centrepiece for me, however, was the panel of four persons with MS, including Liz, who had recovered their health. They were the real experts. Their stories confirmed that recovery was possible—without drugs.

The conference generated a lot of hope and enthusiasm among those who attended. A woman from a distant, small city came to me with half a dozen friends. They suggested another petition as a strategy to encourage research on non-drug approaches to health. I thought it couldn't hurt to try, so that evening I prepared a petition form to circulate the next day. The petition suggested the society dedicate 25% of its research funds to alternative medical research—this would amount to about twenty million dollars. I reduced the proportion to 10% thinking this figure had a better chance of passing at the national level where the final decision would be made. The petition got about 250 signatures, which represented most of the people in attendance.

The provincial board chair was impressed by our effort and by the apparent wide support for the petition's request. The board directed him to take the petition to the national meeting of the society. There it was referred to a research decision-making committee. Off the record I heard that the request and its supporting petition created quite a furor. Members were usually the passive recipients of decisions made by medical experts and staff, not the generators of demands that demonstrated such a lack of respect for conventional medicine.

About three months later the official response came back. Studies that fit into the "alternative" to the drug-based frame would be referred to the small grants committee for approval, which meant only research grants up to thirty thousand dollars could be considered. They would not be subject to the same kinds of scrutiny as other studies were in the "normal" process. I only heard of one study over the following years that applied for funding under this process. The principal investigator was a local neurologist who had specifically refused all invitations to attend our alternative medical conference. He billed his study as an investigation of acupuncture. However, he focused on comparing the acupuncture results to the effects of a drug on only one symptom of MS. I spoke with a doctor of traditional Chinese medicine who had been consulted about the design of the study and the acupuncture treatment. She felt insulted by the process and that the conventional medical researchers had ignored all the usual principles of Chinese medicine. The study results reflected this compatibility problem. They showed that drugs and acupuncture did not work well together, although they both worked equally well alone. The question of side effects was not addressed.

In the middle of planning a second conference, we learned the society had decided that all provincial conferences must cover both conventional and alternative medicine. Although it meant we had to revisit the planning we had already done, on reflection I decided this was a good thing. It meant that future provincial conferences, in any city of the province, also had to include more than just conventional drug-related research.

I worked on planning three such conferences over six years. It was a very satisfying process, but the greatest satisfaction was the opportunity to select and meet our keynote speakers. Many of them had first-hand knowledge of recovery against the odds of conventional thinking.

David Perlmutter is a Florida neurologist. After his wife's life was threatened in a way that baffled his colleagues, he shifted his practice away from symptom-masking drugs and toward nutritional medicine and other approaches that support the body's functions. It was alternative medicine that brought her back to life and health.

Meir Schneider still has less than one percent of intact retina in his eyes, yet he is considered to be fully sighted and holds an unrestricted California driver's license. It was specific forms of rest and exercise for his eyes that restored his ability to see after fifteen years of blindness.

Microbiologist Bruce Lipton told us that science has shown for many years that we need to look to our environment and beliefs for answers to our health problems, not to our genes as both news stories and much MS research tell us.

We need to take charge of our own health, rather than wait for research to find universal answers to health problems. I value these insights and their powerful demonstrations that the beliefs I hold have validity, even if many experts disagree. I continue to write positive stories about holistic approaches to health for the society's newsletters. Of all the topics I've covered, the one that still gets attention is the story that summarizes the work of twelve persons with MS who've told their stories of recovery at the society's conferences.

I hope and pray and work toward the day when I can tell my own story of recovery. Endless abdominal and bum crunches, organic salads and meditation every day don't make life exciting or newsworthy, but they are just some of the things I must do to recover from years in a wheelchair. Until I'm well myself, I collect stories of the people who have recovered. I know my time will come—I just don't know when.

CHOCOLATE

I believe that imagination is stronger than knowledge.
That myth is more powerful than history.
That dreams are more powerful than facts.
That hope always triumphs over experience.
That laughter is the only cure for grief.
And I believe that love is stronger than death.

"The Storyteller's Creed"
from *All I Really Need to Know I Learned in
Kindergarten* by Robert Fulghum

I once heard that all reactions to life could be summed up in one of three words every child knows: yikes, yum and yuk. The 100,000 other words in the English language are just refinements and explications of the basic emotions conveyed by these three words. "Yikes" expresses the primary negative but protective emotion of fear; "yum" and "yuk" are the simplest ways to express the fundamental judgments of good and bad which underlie all of life's experiences.

Sweets were never my favourite treats. As a child I'd always preferred savoury or sour tastes. Fresh baked bread with butter, crackers with cheese, or salt and vinegar potato chips topped my list of favourite comfort foods then. These preferences stayed with me into adulthood.

In my late thirties, my health started to change. I couldn't sleep past 2:00 a.m., and I started reacting badly to many of the foods I'd always eaten without problems. My legs became weak with patches of numbness. When I was forty-two, my doctors told me I had multiple sclerosis, a chronic illness in which physical disability tends to creep up slowly. However, within just two years, I needed a scooter to do my shopping or enjoy a "walk" along the beach or in the forest. I had to use a wheelchair to manage safely in the house as well. Fatigue became my constant companion.

In my first summer of full-blown disability, I adjusted to the trauma of unwelcome life changes by eating great volumes of chocolate every day. Coffee or raspberry-filled chocolates and bars of bitter dark European chocolate were my favourites. I became addicted to both the sugar and the caffeine, but my fatigue was just a memory as long as I kept my body topped up with chocolate.

I only *needed* to eat chocolate once in a twenty-four-hour period to keep the fatigue at bay. However, once I started eating it, I couldn't stop. I understood that sugar didn't give me the "full belly" signal that I'd get if I ate meat and vegetables, so I added chocolate-covered almonds. I nurtured the deluded hope that the almond would give me enough satisfaction so I could reduce the volume I ate in a day.

I always ate my chocolate outside of my home, compulsively, until it was gone. I did this while enjoying the outdoors on my scooter, riding around my neighbourhood or along the beach. I knew my chocolate habit was damaging my health, but I kept the guilt and embarrassment to myself. It was a secret I never told my husband. I felt foolish for forming this addiction and for not being able to kick the habit.

It wasn't that I didn't try. I did, regularly, but without a Chocoholics Anonymous to support my efforts to abstain, I always started eating chocolate again. After twenty-four hours without chocolate, I'd experience withdrawal symptoms in which all I wanted to do was lie curled into a little ball, my muscles tight and my head pounding and clouded with a dismal, overwhelming fatigue. Getting rid of my fatigue was always the excuse I used for starting to eat chocolate again. I always felt there was more to it than that, but I couldn't pinpoint exactly what.

To counterbalance my chocolate consumption, I started following a vegetarian "macrobiotic" diet. I went to monthly macrobiotic meetings and read about how this diet might help restore my health. My macrobiotic books said that both sugar and caffeine were toxic to my liver. I also read that the emotions of anger, irritability and depression result from a stressed liver. *If this is true*, I thought, *my liver must be very stressed as these emotions are constantly with me*. It didn't matter whether a perceived offense was large or small, or whether I wanted to be nice, my irritability seemed to always bubble over. I had once been known for my patience, but that quality had completely vanished. Now I never stopped to reflect before voicing the frustrations that came with my new impatience.

For example, at a take-out café, the attendant handed me a half inch of paper napkins after I asked for one. Instead of thanking the probably bored and overworked teenager for his attempt to be especially helpful to me, I scowled and asked him if I looked like a sloppy eater before leaving the extras on his counter.

One day I was kept waiting a few minutes at the "cash only" checkout till in my local supermarket. The cashier had already rung in the purchases of the customer ahead of me when she realized she only had "plastic" money. Rather than closing the transaction, the cashier sent the errant customer to the bank machine to get cash to pay for her groceries. We both watched as she searched a cavernous purse for some time before coming up with the appropriate card. She apparently keyed in her password incorrectly and had to start over again.

"This is the cash only express till," I said sourly as we watched and waited. "You're supposed to make sure your customers know they need cash before you ring in their purchases. Now you're just standing here picking your nails while your whole lineup waits because you didn't do your job. I bet you wouldn't do this if it was *your* coffee break coming up."

After finally paying for my purchase—a large bar of dark chocolate—I was able to get my caffeine and sugar fix. I ate as I went to my bank to get cash from its Automatic Teller Machine. I inadvertently left with my bank card still in the machine. When I discovered my card was missing two days later, I went to my bank to report the problem. The teller told me they had my card, and that it was the cashier from the supermarket express till who had turned it in. She probably didn't recognize my name, but she would have done me this service in the same hour I had given her a hard time for keeping me waiting in her lineup.

I felt rather sheepish, but I went from the bank to her till and thanked her. I made a joke about my chocolate addiction and how bad I feel when I haven't had my fix for the day. She said she knew exactly how it felt as she was a chocoholic herself. After that, we shared chocolate addiction stories whenever I went through her till. No doubt there was a lineup of frustrated customers behind me, but their waits never mattered to me when I had chocolate on my mind.

Winter came, and I was still eating chocolate every day out in the fresh air on my scooter. The only difference was that it was now often dark before I went out to buy my fix. Because it was frequently raining, I usually just window shopped or rode along the streets of my neighbourhood while I ate my chocolate. One dark and drizzly late afternoon I decided to drive to a nearby park and look out over the inlet to the city lights visible in the distance while I enjoyed my chocolate. I thought I was safe to drive across the grass to the edge of the park where the view was best. I didn't realize I would encounter a series of bumps and ridges along the way, but I kept going when I did and enjoyed my coffee-filled chocolate treats.

Then suddenly, as if in a slow motion dream, my scooter rolled gently onto its side. I tumbled out of my seat onto the damp ground beside the path, fortunately also beside a small puddle of water, not in it. My physical ability was such that I knew I wouldn't be able to get myself back in the scooter alone even if it somehow magically righted itself. My backpack was in my scooter basket, which was now also on the ground. It held my bag of coffee-filled chocolates and was just within my reach.

Michael had often talked of getting me a cell phone for occasions such as the one I found myself in now, but we just hadn't done anything about it yet. As I thought about my predicament, I realized the only people I could have called were the 911 emergency operators as Michael was out of town.

I spent a moment cursing my stupidity. Then I remembered something I had recently read in a book on philosophies from traditional Chinese medicine. It described sweet as a "yin" or "expansive" experience and said that a yearning for sweets is a misunderstood craving for spiritual fulfillment, the ultimate "yin" experience. It seemed an important insight, but it was immediately overshadowed by the insight that lying on the cold, damp side of a knoll in the dark and rain of a December afternoon was not the time for either self-blame or philosophy. Taking a deep breath to return my calm, I reached for a chocolate and looked around to assess my situation.

I was about one hundred metres from the nearest road. Even if a car came along, its driver wouldn't hear me call and certainly wouldn't see me, hidden as I was in a depression beside the path. I could hear the rhythmic bounce and rebound of a basketball in a court I knew to be about one hundred metres from where I was. Next I heard a female voice calling to what I assumed was a dog.

"Here, Laddie. Good boy, Laddie! Fetch, Laddie!"

I could just see their shapes in the distance, but knew that if I could hear them, they'd be able to hear me. They seemed to be moving toward me.

"I need help!" I called out. "I'm on the ground ahead of you, and I can't get up."

After a short pause, a female voice punctuated by the bark of a dog replied, "I can't see you. But keep talking, and I'll try to find you."

"I'm in front of you in a little depression in the ground. I can't walk, and my scooter is tipped on its side," was my relieved reply.

"Don't worry, we'll find you," the voice said through the dark. "Stay with me, Laddie."

Our disembodied conversation continued until I felt a dog's tongue lick my cheek. I'm not fond of dogs, and usually dislike being licked, but I said a silent prayer of thanks for this golden retriever and his mistress.

"Are you hurt?" she asked.

"No," I said, "but I'll need help getting my scooter turned over and then getting back into it."

"I can try," the voice said, "but it looks a bit heavy."

"There's someone on the basketball court. Maybe they can help," I suggested.

"We'll go and check it out. Just wait here. Come, Laddie."

I smiled at the "Just wait here." *Would that I could just get up and disappear*, I thought, but said nothing.

My rescuer returned shortly with the basketball player, a teenage boy wearing only sweatpants and a T-shirt despite the cold and drizzle. Laddie gave me another reassuring lick on my face and wagged his tail.

A young lady's voice said, "I'm Kelly, Laddie's owner. And this is John. You'll have to tell us how to help you."

I directed them first in lifting my scooter back to an upright position. That done, I explained how to turn it on and drive it beside me. With the scooter seat in front of me, I directed Kelly and John on how to help me get my feet and legs in position for standing up. Then they boosted me up with a lift under both my armpits. Standing in front of my scooter, my hands on its armrests, I was able to pivot and sit again.

John left to go back to the basketball court, but Kelly and Laddie stayed with me.

"I'll make sure you get back to the road without another mishap," Kelly said.

Once there, she asked where I lived, and on hearing it was just a half dozen blocks away, Kelly said she'd see me safely home. I learned she was a university student home to visit her family for the Christmas break in her classes.

I initially felt myself to be quite normal, unaffected by the little trauma I had just been through. Yes, I was relieved and happy to be off the cold, damp ground, but nothing more than that. But by the time Kelly, Laddie and I got to my house, I was shaking. A shock reaction had set in. I could only feel grateful for Kelly's watchful presence while I transferred into my wheelchair. As they took their leave, Laddie gave me one last lick and wagged his tail, reassuringly it seemed to me.

I rolled my wheelchair to the gas fire and turned it on to the highest level. When my shaking died down, I changed out of my rain-dampened clothes. I made some chamomile tea and soon began to feel at least close to what passed for normal. As I had so many times before, I vowed to kick my chocolate habit. *The sooner, the better, given today's adventure*, I thought.

It wasn't going to be easy.

I told my naturopathic doctor a few days later that I just wasn't finding the will power I needed to overcome my addiction. Though I asked him to remind me of the details of how damaging chocolate was to my health in the hope this would bolster my determination, he declined, saying that a negative motivation never worked in his experience. He said when I was ready to stop eating chocolate, I would. He left me to deal with my addiction in my own time, in my own way.

I didn't stop eating chocolate immediately, but I reduced the volume and enhanced the quality of what I ate. I started purchasing my daily fix at a newly opened up-market chocolate shop in my neighbourhood. The manager, Paulina, and I became friends. Our lively conversations became as much a draw for my visits as the chocolate. Her interests were writing and acting, and she had a gift for comedy. She always made me laugh. I still ate my chocolate on the move, but I often asked Paulina to cut my purchases into quarters so it felt like I was eating more than I actually was. Then Paulina left her job, and getting my daily chocolate just wasn't the same anymore. The fun was gone.

This seemed like a good time to kick the habit once again. I was determined to give it my best effort. After I survived the first twenty-four hours, it got a little easier. The physical cravings diminished, and the psychological need seemed to be, if not gone, at least a more avoidable priority. One day I was surprised to realize I'd gone a whole week without even thinking about chocolate. Gradually, the thoughts stopped completely.

My birthday came, and someone I hadn't talked with for a while gave me some chocolate as a present. I wasn't even really tempted. I ate one piece as an intellectual exercise. I didn't enjoy it. I found it unpleasantly sweet, and it didn't seem to have much taste. The next day I took the rest of my present to the supermarket cashier with whom I had shared first my irritability and then my chocoholic stories. She seemed delighted.

"Really?" she said in response to my offer. "This is the best kind of chocolate you can buy! Are you sure you want to give all this away?"

I smiled to myself with gratitude and wonder as I realized, *My chocolate yum has turned into a yuk.*

I knew in this moment that my expansive "yin" experiences now came from the ways I nurtured my spirit, and not from what I fed my body.

It felt better than even the best chocolate.

THE BAG LADY

There is a crack in everything.
That's how the light gets in.

Leonard Cohen

t was a rainy December night on the west coast. A woman on a scooter was making a din outside a brightly lit restaurant lounge. Inside, people laughed and conversed while sipping golden brown pints of beer.

A tinny, echoing sound joined the patter of raindrops each time the woman banged an umbrella on the iron railing surrounding a deserted sidewalk patio. The lounge occupants were oblivious to the sights and sounds in the world outside the window. The curious thing was that the woman on the scooter was not wearing a hat or coat or gloves to protect her from the cold and rain. Instead, she was wearing a black plastic garbage bag with rough holes bodged through for her head and arms.

The woman on the scooter was me. As the cold bit deeper, I began to punctuate each umbrella bang on the railing with swear words, muttered not quite under my breath. It seemed to help keep me warm because when I stopped, a shiver ran through my body.

I turned to look at the three steps between me and the warm conviviality on the other side of the half open vertical blinds. As I was unable to stand up from my scooter, each step to the door of the pub may as well have been Mt. Everest. I thought of going to find a business without steps and asking to use the telephone. The nearest was only a block away. I thought of throwing my umbrella at the window. It would at least momentarily satisfy the rage and frustration that was rising toward the surface of my being.

I wondered whether my most blood-curdling scream could penetrate the glow of that warm interior world. I tried telepathy. After all, the man inside occupying my attention was my husband of twenty-five years. But the window seemed an impenetrable barrier even to the thoughts I tried to project.

I let loose one last wallop of the umbrella on the railing and mustered a pale version of a blood-curdling scream, more like a strangled "aaargh." Just at that moment a man opened the door from the inside and moved slowly toward the steps, giving me a startled and somewhat wary look. I must have been an odd sight—a bagged woman on a scooter banging and swearing in the night shadows.

"Do you need help?" the man asked.

The first response that ran through my mind was, *What the bloody hell do you think? That this is my normal Friday night entertainment?* But I responded with calm and gratitude.

"Yes, please. You see the man with the patchwork sweater having a good time with his friends? Would you go tell him that his wife is outside in the pouring rain and needs his house keys?"

I watched as the stranger approached and spoke with my husband, Michael, then turned and pointed out the window. Michael took a last sip of beer, and a moment later he was outside with his coat and keys.

"What happened?" he asked.

"Some genius turned the lock in the front door handle but left the door ajar. When I went into the porch to see Randy off, the door closed. And there I was. No coat, no keys, just my scooter with the plastic bag I use at the swimming pool to protect my seat when I come out. At least I had that."

"You think I did that?" he said.

"I know you did," I said, "but all I want right now are the keys so I can get back in the house and crank up the fire."

Although Michael offered me his coat, I refused on the grounds that that would result in two cold people in one night.

Ten minutes later, I was in my living room with the gas fire cranked to the max. I transferred myself to the couch and pulled a blanket close around me. From this much warmer and calmer vantage point, I could smile at the night's adventures. No doubt the stranger who had gone up those three little steps on my behalf was also home. Perhaps he was laughing, telling his family about the new fashion in raingear he had seen modelled by a swearing, umbrella banging woman on a scooter. I didn't care. I was warm again.

THE WAY TO THE NEIGHBOURS' HEARTS...

Why not go out on a limb, that's where all the fruit is!

Mark Twain

It was never a priority to get to know my neighbours while I was healthy. Work and recreation filled my time, and these activities happened outside of my suburban neighbourhood. I drove to my office half an hour from home five days a week, drove to the gym to exercise three times a week, drove another half an hour to get home, cooked, ate, did a little housework or watched a little TV. After this it was time to go to bed to rest so I could do it all over again the next day. On weekends, I walked in the forest or on the beach and spent time with friends who lived in different suburbs than I did.

Then, over the space of two years, I became a disabled person with a chronic illness living in a wheelchair. I had to stop working and spent a lot of time at home. Michael was out of town on business about two weeks a month. The need to call on someone living close to me for help in case of an unexpected problem—like finding a wasp in my bedroom at night or needing a large bottle of water lifted onto the dispenser—was suddenly a very real possibility. But I didn't really know anyone who lived close to me. I started paying closer attention to the comings and goings of others who lived on my block, but almost all of my neighbours were strangers to me.

An elderly couple lived next door. Michael and I had tea with them one morning a few months after we moved into our new home and seven years before I became ill. Betty and Shirley, who lived directly across from us, always smiled and waved when they saw me, and we occasionally spoke if we were parking our cars on the road at the same time. I sometimes saw a woman with white-blond hair and a Swedish insignia a few houses down in the porch window working in her garden. David and his young son Evan introduced themselves as living at the far end of our block while shopping at a yard sale I had. That was four neighbours I "knew" to a very limited extent out of the twenty-six houses on my block. I started thinking of what it would take to create more of a sense of community in my little corner of this large city.

My first thought was to organize a block party as a way of getting to know my neighbours. But access to the mailboxes of most houses meant climbing stairs, so I knew I'd need a partner for this kind of venture. Michael was too busy to help, so the block party remained just another good idea whose time had not yet come. I would happily have done all the organizing and notifying myself, but Lois, my three-wheeled motorized scooter that provided my mobility outside the house, did not climb stairs. Lois and I travelled miles along the paths in the forest park at the end of our street, and up and down a steep hill to the beach, but even one step was an insurmountable obstacle for her.

Then one winter day I met my neighbour with the white-blond hair and the Swedish insignia as I was leaving my physiotherapist's office. She was leaving another office across the hall at just the same time. I smiled and introduced myself, learning that her name was Ruth. After the first pleasantries, I told Ruth about my block party idea as a way of getting to know more of our neighbours.

"I've been living across the street from you for over seven years already and we've only just met," I said. "At this rate we could both be very old and grey before we get to know anyone else from our block. I think a summer barbeque out on the street seems like a nice friendly way to bring everyone together. What do you think?"

Ruth's face lit up. "I've lived in my house even longer and have had the same thoughts," she said, "but I've just never done anything about it. Maybe I was waiting for a partner."

Ruth and I exchanged phone numbers and the promise to be in touch with one another in early summer to organize the details of a block party.

In June we talked on the phone and chose the third Sunday in July as the date for our first block party. We emailed about the details of the invitation, deciding to make it a potluck lunch from noon until 2:00 p.m. Ruth printed the invitations and decorated each one with crayon drawings of a sun, clouds and seagulls. She delivered a copy to every house a month before the Sunday we'd chosen, and then a second invitation on the Friday before.

The day of our first block party was sunny and warm. Fortunately, Michael was home as Ruth called to ask for help carrying some tables from her basement out onto the grassy verge beside the street. She decorated the tables with colourful covers and put out the paper plates and plastic cutlery I'd bought. Ruth told us she'd found two large lockers filled with fresh salmon outside her door from a neighbour who worked for a fish handling company. He'd phoned to say this was his potluck contribution, although he wasn't able to attend personally. Michael decided to take our barbeque onto the street to cook the fish for anyone who wanted some at the party. He also carried sawhorses and long boards to the ends of the street to block them off and restrict car traffic during our party.

About thirty-five people came out for the occasion. They covered Ruth's tables with a variety of salads, cakes and fruit. They set up lawn chairs under the trees or brought sun umbrellas to create their own shade. One family brought an ice cream maker cooled by liquid nitrogen and provided a science lesson as well as vanilla ice cream to anyone watching the process. It turned out the ice cream maker's owner was a physics professor at the nearby university. Mr. Wu brought several bottles of homemade plum wine which ensured that all who sampled it felt relaxed and happy. Even Ruth's ninety-year-old next door neighbour, Hilda, allowed herself to be coaxed outside where she regaled the assembly with stories of the 1930s when houses were first built on the block. I learned that my house had first been occupied by the family that owned the land on which all the other houses of the block were built.

Small children rode their bicycles along the middle of the road, happy to have their parents watching but not telling them to stay on the sidewalks. A few parents and children already knew one another from meeting at school, but most people were having conversations with their neighbours for the first time.

It turned out that Mr. Wu was a hydrology engineer for thirty years. After retiring, he took up bottle collecting on the nearby golf course and university grounds. He said he needed regular exercise to stay healthy, and this was how the bottle collecting started. Walking every day to collect bottles kept him and his dog Maomao trim and the area free of litter, but Mr. Wu took his good work a step beyond fitness. He'd created scholarship funds with the money he earned from recycling the bottles and cans. He had already created five university scholarships which grew every month after he cashed in his finds.

The good will and good conversation carried on long past two o'clock. Mr. Wu took several photographs of the assembly, making sure that Lois and I were front and centre in every one. Ruth circulated paper and pens to collect phone numbers. There was enough fresh salmon left over for every family to take a side home. When people eventually took their leave, their thanks and smiles told Ruth and me that our street party had been a great success. So did the suggestion that we do it again the next summer.

The block party has become an annual event. After two years of discussions, several families with young children organized a "block watch program" which lowered house insurance costs for everyone. When the block watch police constable spoke at our fourth annual street party, the audience included families of all ages from virtually every house. Parents sat on the warm pavement with their children and neighbours, listening to advice on how to be a good "block watcher." One family even said they'd come home from holidays a few days early to attend the block party.

Fortunately, I haven't needed help very often over the years, which was my motivation for organizing the first block party. But so much more has come from knowing my neighbours. I now feel like I'm part of a real community, even in a middle class suburb in a city of two million people. My neighbours wave and call out to me by name when they see me riding along the street on my scooter. Newcomers speak about a welcome but unexpected feeling of belonging in the neighbourhood after their first summer party.

I feel comfortable asking for surplus apples from neighbours' trees to make cider. Most of my neighbours are still in busy working lives as I once was and are happy to have their homegrown apples put to good use since they don't have time to make anything with them. Mr. Wu likes to share sweets from his favourite Chinese bakery with me, and now I can reciprocate with cider that includes apples which grew on a tree in his yard. And when I do have to call on a neighbour for help, it feels more like calling on a friend.

LEADER OF THE PACK

Life is ours to be spent, not to be saved.

D.H. Lawrence

Ann put her hand deep into her coat pocket looking for the coins she needed to clear her bill at the grocery store. She couldn't feel any stray pennies, but her hand came out full of broken "crunch" bits. Crunch was the treat that her mules, Oh Henry and Sweet Marie, always expected to find when they nuzzled her hand. They had never eaten the chocolate bars they were named after, but Ann felt their blend of nuttiness and sweetness described her mules' characters very well. Crunch was made of compressed hay and oats, and the mules loved it like children love sweets. The mules liked apples and carrots, too, but crunch was their favourite treat.

Trained in nutrition and skilled in management, Ann had applied her knowledge in several different businesses from skin care to bagel bakeries. Through fifteen years of work, Ann's love of animals remained a hobby. But in her early forties, she decided to put her business skills together with her passion for animals and open her own trail riding business. She planned to market her services as a management training opportunity as well as a country holiday option.

Ann knew that, like her mules, horses have no preconceptions, no hidden agendas—food and comfort are their top priorities. A rookie rider has to learn to persuade a nonverbal but very smart creature to not take flight and run for home as its instincts dictate. This requires respect, honesty, consistency and the ability to take responsibility for one's actions. Ann's management experience had taught her that these qualities which one needs to get along with mules or horses are similar to those she'd had to apply in her various jobs. What one must learn to survive a trail ride can then be transferred to human situations. When she saw a television news clip of a trail riding business management training venture opening in California, she decided it was time to make her own dreams a reality.

Ann worked hard on starting her new business—perhaps too hard—striving for perfection as only she could see it. It all seemed like more than her body was willing to handle. Illness struck through an overwhelming fatigue that made it clear she would have to put her trail riding and management training venture on hold for a few months at least.

Ann had experienced numbness and tingling in her right leg for a few years but found it all too easy to ignore. But now her leg no longer seemed to want to carry her forward—or backward, for that matter. Her symptoms didn't improve and eventually led to a diagnosis of multiple sclerosis. Ann's doctors told her she was right to put her business plans aside as her first priority needed to be conserving her energy for the tasks of daily living. Ann grieved the loss of her dreams, but she knew her own competitive nature and need to do things perfectly all too well. As difficult as it was to let go, Ann saw there was no alternative. She had to accept the imposition of health maintenance priorities in her life or live in denial—and she was too much of a pragmatist for that.

Ann rationalized that keeping Oh Henry and Sweet Marie would ensure she got some exercise, if only by their need for her care. But she knew the truth went well beyond providing for their basic needs. Ann had bottle fed them as babies, so she was both mother and pack leader to them. As with her children, she keenly felt the conflict of disciplining the mules when they just wanted to play while she was trying to teach them. She was the top of the pecking order in her mules' world—the leader they obeyed. They returned her affection as only mules can. Mules always remember a new experience and plan accordingly. They will stand and fight rather than run from a challenge.

Because she had trained horses and mules since early adulthood, Ann knew better than anyone that the seemingly ornery beasts are very intelligent despite their popular image. With life-changing health challenges coming her way, Ann's firm conviction was that Oh Henry and Sweet Marie would help her meet them with the confidence and determination of her mules' example. She knew she could apply one of the best training techniques she had always used with mules to herself in her new health situation. Tying one end of a rope to an animal's hind leg and the other around its nose teaches it to stop fighting because it is only fighting itself. If it does kick and try to get the rope off its leg, the rope pressure on the nose tightens and the pain increases. Mules learn this very quickly, and Ann felt this was a good lesson to apply to herself to deal with her changing physical abilities, without the rope.

In the final analysis, Ann sold her horses but kept Oh Henry and Sweet Marie. They were both gaited mules—they always keep one foot on the ground while walking or trotting which meant that she didn't feel any bouncing motion in the saddle. Their mother was a Tennessee walker, a horse known to plantation owners of past centuries for its Cadillac smooth ride. These horses had been trained to always keep one foot on the ground no matter how fast they were moving, and this trait was passed from mothers to offspring. Their father was a donkey, as this cross-species breeding is what it takes to create a mule. Mules themselves are infertile and unable to reproduce.

Ann always felt safe riding on Oh Henry or Sweet Marie. She was sure they would never buck her off as another animal might if it sensed her advancing weakness. Ann never regretted the decision to keep her four-legged companions as she started her new path in life, no matter the financial costs. She began a whole new chapter of mule adventures that kept her smiling.

One day when Ann was out riding Oh Henry, she suddenly felt a most urgent need to pee. The day seemed to be threatening rain, so Ann was wearing her long, tent-like oilskin. There was nowhere to tie Oh Henry while she limped to a bathroom in the tourist town she was riding through, so she decided to tie him to a stump in the park she was in and conceal herself under her oilskin while she squatted and peed. Tourists walked nearby, none the wiser as to Ann's dilemma or her solution.

On another occasion, Oh Henry's role was not quite as passive, and Ann's patience and mule leadership were both put to the test. She had driven Oh Henry to a peaceful location out into the country in her horse trailer. She knew they could ride a trail through farm pastures and bush that would reward Ann with vistas of great beauty and Oh Henry with lush grass to eat as they went. Ann had a plan for how to get on Oh Henry even though her right leg was not strong enough to swing it over his back from a standing position. She planned to create a V-shaped channel by turning her truck to the limit of its trailer hitch clearance. She'd tie Oh Henry to the side of the trailer and use her arm strength to boost herself onto the truck's protruding fender. From there she'd be able to swing even her uncooperative leg over Oh Henry's back. That was the plan, anyway.

Ann positioned Oh Henry next to the truck's fender and tied his reins to the trailer. She limped back to the fender where the next phase of the plan was to boost her bottom a few inches up onto the fender. Usually her arm strength only needed a small amount of support from her legs to execute a manoeuvre like this. Today, however, she found her legs were too tired to provide even the small proportion of the effort it would take to get her 135 pounds up onto the fender.

Perhaps it was her own stubbornness that gave Ann her great love for her often equally stubborn mules. She needed this quality today as she tried to get herself up onto the fender from several angles. Oh Henry gave her an occasional glance but otherwise occupied himself with chomping the long grass in front of him. Eventually Ann's efforts got her where she wanted to be—perched on her truck's fender and poised to swing her leg over Oh Henry's back. After the Herculean effort it had taken to get on to the fender, Ann decided to have a little rest before attempting the next move.

She closed her eyes briefly and enjoyed the warmth of the sun on her face. When she opened her eyes a few seconds later, Oh Henry was no longer in position for her to mount him from the fender. He had pulled his reins out from the trailer and moved a few steps away from the truck toward a juicier patch of grass. It meant Ann's mounting plan was no longer possible.

"Ohhh, Henry!!! What have you done?" Ann exclaimed in exasperation and dismay.

She knew she did not have the reserve for the simple job of sliding down to the ground, repositioning Oh Henry, and then boosting herself back up onto the fender to be able to swing her leg over his back for the ride that was the purpose of this whole adventure. Ann closed her eyes again and felt the heat of tears of frustration close behind her eyelids. That was all it took to bring her trainer's knowledge that she was the leader of her mule pack to the top of her consciousness. She wasn't sure how—yet—but she would find a way to assert her dominance to get Oh Henry to come back to the position in which he had to be for her to mount him. She intended to enjoy her ride no matter what it took to get it started.

Ann's trainer experience and patience helped return her voice to an authoritative calm. She knew that repetition was the key to having her commands obeyed.

"Oh Henry, get back in position. Here beside the truck. Right in front of me. Now." Ann pointed to the ground in front of her legs as she spoke.

Oh Henry glanced back over his shoulder, long blades of grass protruding from the sides of his mouth as he continued chewing.

"Oh Henry, get back in position. Here beside the truck. Right in front of me. Now."

Oh Henry looked back at Ann again, and this time she felt she could see the *Well, if I really have to* look on his face. It told her he was getting ready to obey.

"Oh Henry, get back in position. Here beside the truck. Right in front of me. Now," she commanded again.

It worked! Oh Henry moved a few steps back toward Ann, positioning himself perfectly for her now somewhat rested leg to make its swing over her saddle. Her left foot found the stirrup immediately in front of it. She leaned forward in her saddle and took the reins in her hands.

"Gidd'ap, Oh Henry. There's a lot more sweet grass over the next hill. You'll see. You won't go hungry."

Ann rubbed his neck affectionately as they set off, watching his big ears moving in time with his feet. She smiled, feeling pride in the fellow creature she thought of as a friend and in the proof that she was still the leader of her mule pack.

She knew that she learned as much from her mules as she had ever taught them. She thought the lessons of patience and finding new ways to accomplish routine tasks in changed circumstances gave her the more valuable end of the bargain. Her trail riding school was a reality after all, although she was its only student. Its mule teachers were as cryptically wise as ever—as long as she stayed receptive to their lessons.

SWEATER MEMORIES

I am what I am, and what I am needs no excuses.

Shirley Bassey

decided to go shopping with a friend on a sunny September day to escape the sounds and smells of garden renovations in my backyard. I found a beautiful, natural cotton sweater with a cable knit pattern on the body and round, marble-sized baubles made of the same yarn stitched on the sleeves in one of my favourite stores. The sales clerk told me the sweater would be going on sale in the next week, so I decided to come back and get it then.

My friend and I sat in the sun with iced tea after the shopping. I commented that the baubles on the sweater I liked reminded me of marbles. Free associating, I then commented further that I had played marbles in my childhood. It had been one of my favourite games. My first friend in life, my older sister's son Lyle, taught me. My friend seemed interested, so I continued the reverie.

I was a farm kid. All my siblings were a lot older than me, and, in fact, I had a niece a year older than me. Lyle was six months younger, and I lived for the visits with my sister's family. My older siblings would let Lyle and I play with them, but for me alone they would find excuses to avoid having to babysit.

Hide-and-seek. Kick the can. Run-sheep-run. These were the games of a country childhood in the fifties. After Lyle taught me how to play marbles, I started to collect them. I had a big syrup can full of the small ones, the size of the sweater sleeve baubles. I had some bigger ones as my shooters too. Lyle knew the names for all the different patterns on the marbles. Cat's eyes. Crystals— red, blue, green or clear. Steelies. Peewees. This was just one of the reasons I loved Lyle. Life could get a little dull on the farm with only cats for friends. But around Lyle, life was always fun. I especially loved it when I got to stay with him at my sister's house in the city.

It was on one of these occasions that I got the only spanking of my life. My mother didn't believe in spankings. She was a pacifist. Lyle lived just two blocks from a park with swings, a merry-go-round, a slide and other entertainments to delight a child's heart. But his main interest at the park was the sandpit. He had a collection of toy tractors, trucks and other miniature equipment and buildings. He created whole worlds with these—highways, gas stations and towns. He made the sounds of his equipment with his mouth, spit dribbling down the dirt on his chin. Found articles like a piece of cardboard or a bottle cap became a bridge deck or a stop sign on a popsicle stick. There were no "reality limits" to the possibilities in Lyle's worlds.

One summer evening, Lyle and I raced from the supper table to the park without asking permission. The adults thought we were downstairs watching television. Lyle's brother and sister got bored with TV and came to the park a while later. Just when the roads and bridges and gas stations were almost complete, Lyle's father arrived. He was not happy. He insisted we all go home with him. I knew there was going to be consequences even though I didn't know the word yet. At home, all four of us were given a choice to help us remember the error of our actions that night: stay home and go to bed. Now. The other choice was a spanking, but then we could go back to the park.

The sun would still be out for hours, and it was one of the best velvety-warm prairie summer evenings, the kind you really must savour, the kind that carries you through a prairie winter. The smells of the flowers tickled your nose as you went by them. The sounds of the bumblebees filled your ears. They were still busy collecting pollen to make the honey Lyle and I liked on our toast with peanut butter.

As far as Lyle was concerned, there was no choice. He went to get the strap. His brother and sister headed for their bedrooms. I didn't know what was in store, but I knew I was with Lyle. Whatever it was like to be spanked, going back to the park was worth it. The spanking left my bum tingling, but then we were out the door and running. There was a city, a world, to finish.

I smiled as I told my friend these memories as we finished our iced tea. Thinking the garden renovations would be complete, we left for my house. As soon as we arrived, I smelled mould and knew I was in for trouble. It wasn't the typical mould smell I recognized from after a rain. I was hypersensitive to a whole host of airborne pollutants, but moulds were the worst at that time. I had worked very hard to clean up the old house where I lived, and the mould culture test results showed that my one-hundred-year-old house was as free of moulds as a new apartment.

Michael sheepishly walked to the car to warn me. He and a friend had decided to cut down the old apple tree in our backyard while I was out, and because it was a warm day, all the windows in the house were open. The mould smell was everywhere. Inside and out. Michael said he had no idea how rotten the tree was inside before he started cutting into it. Everyone found the smell offensive, and it gave them headaches and made them achy.

My capacity to move declined almost immediately. I used a scooter or a wheelchair to get around, but this was a whole new story. I was effectively paralyzed within two hours even though I stayed outside, away from the stump and its cuttings. We decided to call an ambulance.

At the emergency ward, the doctors agreed the best place for me was in the hospital for the time being. I had never been in hospital before, but I ended up staying ten long days.

Thirty hospital meals.
Two hundred and forty hours of senile roommate mumbling.
Too many rings for the bedpan.
Six bouquets of flowers.
Five washes in the bed.
Five showers (two of them attended by male nurses).
A dozen visitors.
And many other things I've chosen to forget.

Then I was finally home again. The air had cleared. The wood stumps were gone. After all the home care arrangements were settled, I called the shop to find out if the sweater with the sleeve baubles was still on sale. It was. But the sale ended the next day, and my size was not available in the local store.

I decided I would take a taxi, at least one way, to get the sweater at another store before the sale ended. Even though there was a nice fountain and gardens to visit, I had definitely suffered from cabin fever in the hospital. Whenever it rained, the mould on the soil bloomed. In my already weakened state, the garden became too toxic for me to tolerate, so I stayed inside in the stale air of the ward. These restrictions made me keen to go out shopping for the sweater with the good memories on the sleeves even though it would have been better for my health to stay home and rest.

I took a taxi to the store with a plan to ride my scooter home along the concrete sidewalks. It was a brisk but sunny autumn day. I craved some outdoor air. It hadn't rained for three days, so I felt my body should be able to handle it—at least from the mould point of view.

Even before I arrived at the store, though, another problem surfaced. I had to pee. Pretty badly too. The store sales attendants greeted me and offered their assistance in any way I might require. I asked if there was a washroom with a grab bar on the wall. I couldn't believe my luck. There was. They would just need to clear out a few boxes, they said.

I had encountered this before. Disabled washrooms have so much tempting space and they're hardly ever used, or so able-bodied people seem to think. Restaurants often store spare tables and chairs in them. Or floor cleaning equipment. Just because there's technically a disabled washroom in an establishment doesn't mean it's actually accessible to someone in a wheelchair.

It was very hot where I waited for the washroom clearing, and I picked up on a strong aroma of formaldehyde—another pollutant to which I reacted, but not nearly as badly as to moulds. I always had a headache after encountering it, and my balance and co-ordination got poorer than they already were. It was the reason I usually limited my shopping trips to stores where I knew the ventilation was good or the doors were kept open to the street. I knew a lot about formaldehyde, just like I knew about moulds. Formaldehyde is used to insect-proof fabrics. I knew a couple of clothing store sales attendants who always felt sick on the days they worked and fine on their days off. Their complaints had a real physical basis. It wasn't just that they hated their jobs, as some people liked to say. It was the formaldehyde.

I waited with my legs crossed tight together. The boxes just kept coming out of the disabled washroom. The point came when I knew I wouldn't be able to hold on much longer, so I told the store attendant I would manage with the box clearing at the stage it had reached. I would be able to get my scooter past the last of them, and I declined the offers of assistance. Just in case. I preferred to embarrass myself in private.

I drove in. I did some manoeuvring to get close enough to reach the grab bar and pull myself up, and I couldn't reach to close the outside door from the same position. I would have to pee with it open. I knew I didn't have time to drive back close enough to shut the door, but it seemed like a quiet part of the store's stockroom.

I can only speculate as to exactly what happened next.

Knowing I had just milliseconds before the pee floodgates opened, I pulled myself up and forward. Perhaps a little too vigorously. Perhaps it was the formaldehyde. My body fell against the wall, and I started to pee with my trousers still up around my waist. I sat down on the toilet. Hard. My left arm was stuck between the wall and the grab bar. I left my arm as it was for a bit and tried to collect myself. It was incredibly hot. And the formaldehyde was very potent. I was sweating. My head was aching. My tongue felt thick and dry. I could feel the bite of tears behind my eyes.

I tried to pull my arm out from behind the grab bar, but it wouldn't fit through. It just hurt when I moved it. My trousers were still dripping. With my right arm, I reached behind me into my scooter basket. I always carried a garbage bag or two with me, and I never knew when or how they would come in handy. Like now. I spread it out over the cloth seat but not too wide. I didn't want others to be able to see that I was sitting on a garbage bag because they might guess my sordid little secret.

I tried a few more times to pull my arm out from behind the grab bar, which only increased the pain. I decided I would have to go public and call for help. My voice sounded a bit fluttery. My tongue seemed coated with slime. I called again. And again. Nothing happened. No response.

Then the anger response kicked in. Anger at myself for getting into this predicament. Stuck to the wall. Sodden trousers and underwear. *Damned if I'll ask for help in this state*, I thought. *I got my arm in here. There has to be a way to get it out too. Take a deep breath. Clear your head. Think.*

I realized I would have to push my arm toward the wall before I tried to lift it out from behind the bar, which would maximize what little wriggle room there was. Maybe it helped that I was sweating from the heat and my arm was damp, but by pushing into the wall and then lifting, I got my arm out. I felt just a little pain that was far overshadowed by relief.

I stood and squooshed down onto the garbage bag on my scooter seat. I reached into my backpack for a paper hanky to wipe the sweat off my face, smoothed my hair and smiled. Then I went back out into the world of the store where life had continued as normal, oblivious to the drama in the storeroom cum disabled washroom.

The sales attendant got the sweater I wanted to try. The medium fit perfectly. The bag under my bottom didn't show as I turned this way and that, admiring the sweater. The attendant smiled encouragement absolutely none the wiser as to my bathroom adventures.

I paid for the sweater and stored it in my scooter basket. I needed the fresh air that riding my scooter home would give me even though I felt exhausted and my head was throbbing from the formaldehyde.

I smiled to myself. Only I knew the trauma I had just come through. The store attendants would continue to see me as a normal person. The only thing that made me different was that I just couldn't walk at this time. I could go back to that store anytime with my head held high.

And I did love my new sweater with the good memories in the sleeve baubles. Only now it had a whole new set of memories indelibly etched in my mind. I now could only think of it as my peed pants sweater.

My shoulder and elbow were still sore days later. When the physiotherapist came to my house to treat me with ultrasound therapy, she asked how I had hurt myself. She thought it an odd injury. I just said, "You wouldn't believe it if I told you." I had a smile on my face. I was wearing my new sweater.

THE FEELING OF MOVEMENT

We cannot direct the wind, but we can adjust the sails.

Anonymous

Deborah was a farm kid, the firstborn in a family of nine. She was named after her mother's favourite Hollywood actress, Deborah Kerr. But in the no-nonsense way of people with more work than time, everyone except her grandmother and teachers shortened her name to "Deb."

Deb's family fed itself and their animals off the land of their mixed farm. This meant every family member was responsible for some chore. No boys arrived until child number five, so the girls learned to do what was considered men's work on other farms. Being the oldest, Deb became the chief truck and tractor driver, she mowed and baled hay, hauled grain at harvest time and completed any other farm work that needed a driver. The smell of newly cut hay meadows made summer Deb's favourite season even though it was one of the busiest.

But the pull of love took Deb away from her family's farm. She married Thomas Winter, and together they raised their own family of six sons, four of their own and two foster sons. They lived on Tom's home First Nations reserve a few miles outside of Kamloops, a small city on a dry plain between two mountain ranges. Tom was a truck driver. Deb worked in an office in addition to taking care of her home and family, but her passion was her hobby farm. She raised llamas and chickens and grew her own vegetables.

In her mid thirties, Deb developed intermittent numbness in her left arm and other signs of a mysterious chronic health problem. She carried on working as a research file clerk as long as she could, but eventually her energy levels became too unpredictable. Some time after she stopped working, Deb added a sweet natured (and only slightly smelly) pot-bellied pig to her farm. She named the pig Emily, her favourite girl's name.

Deb drove a three-quarter ton farm truck to and from work even with her numb left arm. The truck had a standard gearshift, but Deb always managed safely since shifting was a right arm function. She found steering was easy enough with her left arm, even on days when it was very numb.

Tom was more concerned than Deb, especially when his work started to keep him away from home for several days at a time. Eventually even Deb had to admit that managing the clutch and the lack of power steering in the three-quarter ton were becoming too much for her strength and co-ordination. Relieved, Tom began to look for a reliable second hand automatic gear shift car for Deb. Around this time, Deb's numbness expanded and sometimes also affected her feet.

A few days after Tom had licensed the new car he'd bought for Deb, she needed to make a trip to Kamloops to get some supplies the veterinarian had suggested she have on hand. Emily was pregnant, and Deb wanted to do whatever she could to make sure the precious pig had an easy time delivering her first litter. Deb was very excited about the impending birth. It felt almost like a first grandchild to her.

Along the highway access road on the way to Kamloops, she saw a neighbour, Iris Longbow, hitch-hiking. Deb didn't know Iris well, but she knew that while the early morning summer air was still cool, it would soon be swelteringly hot—too hot to walk to Kamloops and back. She picked Iris up, and they drove into town without much conversation after the initial pleasantries. Deb enjoyed and appreciated the easy manoeuvrability of her little car more than she thought she would.

Although Iris was quiet and shy, she did tell Deb that her family was haying that day, and she intended to buy beer to keep her husband and his brothers working through the afternoon heat. In Kamloops, Deb parked in a location that was central to both the veterinary supply store and the liquor store, and she and Iris went their separate ways.

Back at the car half an hour later, Deb and Iris stowed their purchases in the trunk and buckled themselves into their seat belts for the journey home. Reversing out of the parking spot, the new car was very sluggish. Deb felt she was pressing the gas pedal as normal, but the car only just crawled out onto the road. Once there, Deb shifted into drive and again pressed her foot down to accelerate. This time they didn't move at all. Fortunately there was no traffic, and the slope of the road gave them just enough momentum to get back into their parking spot.

Thinking that it wasn't like Tom to misjudge the reliability of a car, Deb's brain started running through all the things she should check to try to find the problem. She turned the engine off and it restarted with nothing appearing to be amiss. But still she could not get any acceleration.

Deb switched the car off again and told Iris to wait while she got out and checked under the hood. Everything looked clean and normal; no wires seemed to be loose, and Deb couldn't see anything obvious that would explain the lack of acceleration. Deb got back in the car, started the engine and tried again to back out of the parking stall onto the road. Still no luck. Iris looked a bit puzzled in the passenger seat, but she just waited patiently while Deb wracked her brain and muttered to herself.

Deb felt a momentary flash of nostalgia for her old three-quarter ton truck. Beast that it was to manoeuvre, at least it had always been reliable. She started to think about who she could call to check the car for her. Tom had left on a trip to Alaska that morning and wouldn't be home for nearly a week. Deb sometimes went with him on such trips, catching up on her rest in Tom's sleeper as he drove and eating someone else's cooking at the truck stop restaurants. But this time none of her sons could take care of her animals. Besides, Deb wanted to be home when Emily gave birth, and that could be any time now. Deb also found the heat draining this summer, so all in all, she'd decided home was the best place to be.

For just a moment, Deb's independence failed and she wished Tom was home so she could call him to solve her problem. Then her thoughts turned to the very pregnant Emily. Deb hoped she was still resting peacefully in the shade. Deb decided to take one last try, so she put it into gear and again pressed her foot down to accelerate. Again nothing happened. She pressed harder. Still nothing. Deb told Iris she thought they'd have to leave the car and hitch-hike back to the reserve together before the sun got too high overhead.

Keeping her eyes downcast, Iris told Deb quietly and politely that the car might work better if she actually tried putting her foot on the gas pedal instead of on the floor beside it. With a rush of embarrassed realization, Deb looked and—sure enough!—her foot was on the car floor *beside* the accelerator! No wonder the car hadn't moved (or even made any engine revving sounds, now that she thought about it). She had pressed her foot, but not the accelerator, to the floor. It was one of those numb days and she hadn't even realized it. Deb threw her head back and laughed until the tears flowed.

As they drove home, Deb told Iris about Emily's pregnancy and about the episodic numbness in her hands and feet. Explaining helped Deb get over feeling like a complete fool. She felt it was most likely her concern for Emily that had made her oblivious to the fact that her feet were numb.

Iris remained impassive throughout Deb's story of her health challenges and apologies for the delays, saying only, "A ride is a ride."

Deb recognized Iris's calm acceptance of what is in the face of problems. She had seen it in Tom and his family, too, and it was one of the reasons she loved them. Knowing she would be home with Emily in a few minutes, Deb breathed deeply and relaxed. The smell of newly mown hay filled her heart with joy and serenity as she sped back to the reserve.

THE INNER BITCH

He only deals in science—double blinded…
I've gone home to my world, where experience rules,
where sense can be made, of any symptom,
where any body is a redeemable case.

Two Worlds by Barbara Alldritt

'**ve** heard there are people called breatharians. They're sort of like vegetarians, except they get all their nutritional needs from the air they breathe, not from vegetable matter they eat. For a time, I thought seriously about looking into what it would take to become a breatharian. Eating, whether animal or vegetable, always felt like walking through a minefield. Every choice I made was fraught with perils. Foods in my "safe" category moved into the "red flag" category with lightning speed. I did my best to eat on a four-day choice rotation plan, but I soon did not have enough variety left in my safe vegetable category even for this.

After eating, I often had to spend the rest of the day with poor balance, altered sensory capacity in my hands, cold legs and feet, a foggy brain that just wanted my body to lie on the couch with no regard for commitments, urinary urgency, disabling fatigue, or unexplained irritability that could turn to anger on the snap of a finger. There were other problems as well, but you get the picture. If I made the wrong choice about what to eat just to survive, never mind for pleasure, life became, as they say, *hell on wheels*. And they aren't referring to my wheelchair.

I'd always been a practical person, a problem solver, not prone to spending too much time feeling sorry for myself. I believed that if I used my clear-headed time to investigate these food sensitivities, I'd be able to resolve them.

After several allergy tests, the doctor confirmed that the range of foods I could safely eat had reduced precipitously. I felt sure that the process that was causing the allergies was ongoing, and that the overall number of my "safe" foods was continuing to decline.

I heard about a woman with a doctoral degree in nutrition who'd had some success with children's sensitivities. I waited with hope through the two months it took to get in to see her as a new patient, so I was very disappointed that her only advice was to continue to avoid those foods with which I already knew I had problems. She offered me no new insights on the underlying cause of my problems, no new solutions, and no hope for recovery. She did, however, acknowledge in her distinctive South African accent that my problems were "extreme."

After this disappointment, friends told me about a medical doctor with a master's degree in nutrition, a rather unusual combination in my experience. His office was in my neighbourhood. So I made an appointment to discuss heavy metal poisoning, a problem I had just come to understand might be what was affecting my health. His somewhat unconventional interest in nutrition seemed promising. By now my burgeoning health problems had brought extensive experience with the medical system. I was already more than a little disillusioned with repeatedly hearing, "No, we don't understand what is causing your problems," and, "No, there is nothing we can offer to help you."

Unfortunately, I got more or less the same message with a bit of a twist from him. My understanding of the role of heavy metal poisoning in my health challenges was, admittedly, a little hazy at the time. I did, however, have a very clear conception of how the poisoning would have come about in my case.

After listening to my story, he responded by reiterating the standard North American medical line about mercury being perfectly safe in one's amalgam tooth fillings. My story of the problem starting only after having a mixture of metals—gold as well as the mercury amalgams—put in my mouth didn't "cut any ice" with him. He challenged me to bring him research references which showed he was wrong. He stated he was well-informed, that he made a point of being on top of the latest medical research, and if there really was a problem with mercury amalgam dental fillings in conjunction with gold, he would be aware of it.

I left the doctor's office feeling more sure than ever that my cynicism about conventional medical education was rational. His narrow and arrogant perspective confirmed it. I already knew that key research showing possible problems with mercury in one's teeth had been done in a city where I used to live. I also knew that having mixed metals in one's mouth raised the electric potential and sped the release of the weakest metal, mercury, overwhelming the body's capacity to store or remove the metal from the body by normal channels. I also knew that in some European countries putting mercury in people's teeth, particularly children's, was already prohibited. The metals had been out of my teeth for two years already, but I wasn't sure what my next step should be. And I was fighting health challenges on too many fronts to feel confident I'd be able to do the required research quickly enough to avoid further loss of function.

I went home to rest, wondering why I'd bothered to ask for his perspective. I'd heard it all before, but hope springs eternal, as they say. My hope was that he'd tell me what I'd have to do to get the mercury out of my body, but his response was just another indication that I'd have to muster the energy to find my own answers to resolve my unique blend of problems.

Three or four months later, my food sensitivities were still severely limiting all my life choices. I hadn't had the energy to do my own research and felt I was only just surviving. My past disappointments with the doctor were just a dim memory. So having been reminded of his expertise in food and nutrition by yet another well-meaning acquaintance, I decided to put aside my doubts and give him another chance.

It was a dark and rainy late winter afternoon when I rode my scooter to his office. My thinking felt foggy. I had been fatigued all day despite having spent several hours lying down resting. My hands felt thick and numb, and my balance was poor. All in all, it was a normal day for me at that time.

The doctor chose to see me in a little room that was cramped with the usual paraphernalia one finds in a doctor's office: a desk, an examination table, some chairs and a shelf of books. There was only just enough space for the two of us. Although I am only five foot, two inches tall and weighed about 110 pounds at the time, my scooter fills enough space for four people my size (or two very large ones). I had seen him in a spacious conference room on my previous visits. I had to back my scooter into the consulting room to be able to see him without having to turn my head awkwardly and look over my shoulder. There wasn't enough room to swing the door closed, so our voices would be audible to the reception desk and the waiting area. I could hear the hum of conversations taking place there whether I wanted to or not.

The doctor opened the consultation by asking how he could help me. I told him about my food sensitivities and about how they affected my body functions. I talked about how difficult it was trying to live with such limited food choices, and about my fears that the problem was just getting worse. He asked what I could eat without reacting. I listed the roughly ten foods I could eat without triggering problems at that time. His response stunned me.

"You will get adequate calories, all the macronutrients, the proteins, fats and carbohydrates, and all the micronutrients, all the vitamins and minerals you need even if you limit your food intake to those you can tolerate. You really don't have a problem with your nutrition."

"What about all the foods I've become allergic to?" I asked. "Is there anything I can do to reverse these reactions? Because, like I said, my sensitivities seem to be expanding. I'd really like to be able to have a little more variety in my diet. I can't ever eat out with friends or anything."

"Well, that's not a problem I can help you with," he said. "You *are* getting adequate nutrition from your food, even if you aren't getting pleasure. That's another question, and that I can't help you with. Maybe you should see a psychologist. Or look at taking up a hobby."

My background irritability turned to anger. I felt it rising on a flood of hot, blind desire to be out of this person's presence. He had his feet outstretched in front of him, in the path of my exit. I switched my scooter on and headed for the door without speaking. I felt a satisfying bump as my back wheel ran over his foot. I didn't stop, didn't apologize.

In the cool, damp air outside of the doctor's office, I took some deep breaths to try to bring my anger under control. My hands were shaking and my face felt flushed and hot. I thought to myself *Towanda was right when she said sometimes all a woman has left is being a bitch.* Twonda was played by Kathy Bates in the movie *Fried Green Tomatoes.* She repeatedly drove her car into the car that had just stolen a parking spot for which she'd waited, sweating in the hot sun. I rode my scooter home, feeling no remorse about running over his foot.

My body isn't stupid, I fumed. *It doesn't do this to me without reasons. I'll just have to find them myself. No matter how long it takes.*

I let out the intense emotion my anger generated by writing a poem. It was the first such creative effort since high school. It felt good, even if the result wasn't. I called it *Two Worlds*. It expressed my growing conviction that whatever the people of science or medicine told me, I was a treatable case. I would not spend the rest of my life avoiding 98% of nature's bounty because the "experts" had been educated into ignorance. There were solutions for my health problems; I just hadn't found them yet. But I would.

FIDELITA, TILLY & SOFIE

In reality, sir, the only real freedom that anyone
actually finds is within the confines of one's own
mind and spirit.

> Courtroom address by environmental activist
> Betty Krawczyk in *Lock Me Up or Let Me Go*.

Renaissance scientist René Descartes posited
the separation of spirit from matter during the
seventeenth century. Science took over matter and
the church got spirit. In the twenty-first century, the
talk is about reintegrating the matter of body with spirit.
Athletes, as well as science, now show us that the power
of mind, the third aspect of who we are, influences the
outcome of every human endeavour. So in any attempt
to change or improve, all three aspects of the self—body,
mind and spirit—must be addressed. It's become almost
a cliché.

Mystics cultivate spirit through meditation, prayer or
various rigorous controls of the body. Athletes mentally
rehearse perfect physical performance. Countless
books, lectures and workshops address this process of

reintegrating body, mind and spirit. For me, however, it just seemed to happen as a natural response to the challenges of ill health.

Over the space of a very short time, what was diagnosed as multiple sclerosis put me in a wheelchair, and my doctors believed I would remain in it for the rest of my life. This idea and the very real health challenges I lived with every day were a serious limitation to the joys of life as I had known them. It went well beyond being unable to walk.

Take eating, for example. A body needs food every day or it starts to fade away. The tastes and textures of food alone usually provide at least some enjoyment. Sharing one's food with interesting company often multiplies the pleasure. And the priest turned writer, Thomas Moore, says eating feeds the soul if it is done with mindfulness and attention to beauty in the presentation of even the simplest food. This was my experience as well, but after I contracted MS it seemed like everything I ate gave me more problems. I couldn't eat what my family and friends ate anymore. It didn't matter how mindfully I chewed, or whether the food was presented on a paper plate or my best china. Every time I ate, I felt worse than when I started.

Even bok choy, I discovered, disorganized my balance and made me feel fuzzy headed, as well as giving me serious pain from muscle spasms. I hated bok choy and only ate it because I thought it was good for me. I wasn't sorry to give it up when I discovered it was a culprit in my health problems.

However, the list of foods I could eat without causing adverse health effects was becoming very short. It only included turkey, fish and vegetables—organic ones at that—and every now and then some millet or a red potato. It had to be a red one. But my stiffness and pain from muscle spasms always got worse when I ate.

Then I discovered that not eating cabbage, of all things, seemed to help me feel better. It wasn't just cabbage, as it turned out. It was any vegetable with organic sulfur in it. Onions, garlic, cabbage, broccoli, cauliflower, asparagus, leeks, kale, Brussels sprouts and turnips. They all have sulfur in them. And yes, bok choy is in this list too.

You may well ask: What does that leave? Well, it leaves lettuce, chard, peas, beans, carrots, celery, eggplant, peppers and tomatoes. But I was allergic to beans, carrots, celery, eggplant, peppers and tomatoes. That only leaves lettuce, chard and peas. But the spasm and fuzzy headedness were bad enough to make me happy to live with eating just a protein and a three vegetable salad. For breakfast, lunch and dinner. Seven days a week.

With my food so lacking in entertainment value, I started watching TV while I ate even though it probably wasn't very good for my mind or soul. I liked documentaries, and watched a series on the twentieth-century dictators that included Hitler, Mao, Tito, Castro and Stalin. It struck me that my body was the supreme dictator in my life because if I didn't do what it wanted, it had ways of making me wish I had!

The first time the thought occurred to me, I called my body "little Stalin" but immediately relented. Stalin was about as nasty a dictator as has ever lived in any century. I needed a more benign comparison. Castro seemed the best choice. He took power to make life better for his people, and he did in many ways. He was a much more benign dictator than the self-aggrandizing butcher, Stalin. Yes, I decided, Castro was the best choice as a namesake for my body.

But referring to my female body as Castro or Fidel felt wrong. It would have to be feminized. Since the way to do this in Spanish is to add the suffix "ita," my body became Fidelita. It felt right. And it let me feel less crazy when asking my body what it wanted from me.

I decided I should learn to speak my body's language. It's called applied kinesiology, or muscle testing, and was recommended by many of the alternative health practitioners I consulted. I found it a bit like a computer language in that the only valid questions are those with "yes" or "no" answers. I learned to hold the question I wanted my body to answer in my mind. Questions like whether a substance I held in my armpit was acceptable to Fidelita. If my linked thumbs and index fingers held strong when I tried to pull them apart, she was answering "yes" to my question. If they pulled apart easily, her answer was no.

I learned to always ask Fidelita first if she found a medication I was thinking of taking acceptable. And I always asked her about new foods I wanted to try. If the first answer was "yes," I would ask about medication dose or how often she would allow me to eat the food. I always complied. I'd had enough of the torture chamber!

I was always polite to Fidelita, too, saying thank you for every answer she gave. I hoped it would make her more inclined to overlook a few small indiscretions, like the odd chocolate or bag of potato chips. It seemed to work. Fidelita started to release my muscles from the spastic grip she had previously held them in and allow my head to stay clear after eating.

I tried telling a friend about Fidelita once. But rather than seeing the humour in it or the sanity it gave my impossible challenges, my friend raised the spectre of schizophrenia. I knew all about that hell, since my sister lived in it. So although I didn't think the comparison was valid, I decided to keep my relationship with Fidelita private, at least for a while.

Once Fidelita and I were working well together, I started to think that my emotional self could use a name, too, because it possess some distinct characteristics of its own. The first names I thought of were male again. Genghis. Attila. I wanted a name that would convey the reality that my emotions often seemed out of control; bent on destruction. They did not allow me the peace, joy and serenity I craved. The historical associations tell something of the story. I often found myself snapping at hapless checkout counter clerks or completely bent out of shape by some small thing that didn't please my tidy nature, like newspapers left littering the couch.

I spent my birthday depressed and crying even though nothing in my life had changed and people were trying to be nice to me. I knew Chinese medicine understands the emotions of irritability, anger and depression to be caused by liver stress. So I just turned up the volume on Tracy

Chapman's "Gimme One Reason." To calm my being I knew I'd have to talk to Fidelita to figure out what was stressing my liver and creating my mental volatility.

I didn't know enough about either Genghis Khan or Attila the Hun to resolve the name issue for my emotional self. I kept meaning to go to the library to do some research, but life just seemed too short to spend an afternoon studying violent warlords. In the end, I decided on Tilly. It was close to Atilla, and I remembered my father talking about a woman he'd known in the 1930s called Tilly. She'd lived alone, dressed in gunny sacking and chased off curious kids with a .22 rifle, he'd said. *That seems to fit*, I thought. My emotions were often unable to tolerate people or probing, and all too often were rough as sackcloth. So working with Fidelita to manage my liver stress helped Tilly stay quiescent. I had integrated body and mind without even trying!

Even through the worst of times, I was aware that I was not just my body or the emotions for which I so often had to apologize. Just the fact that I knew this proved my case as far as I was concerned, and it seemed to me it was evidence that I had a wise spirit. Rough as my health problems had been with all the losses they had imposed on me, I valued the lessons I was learning.

I no longer feared death, for example. I knew for certain that the gods were watching me because the longer and darker the tunnel they put me through, the brighter the light of the spiritual peace at the other end.

"So hit me with your best shot, god," I learned to say to them. "I'm ready! Let's get through it!"

And when I started to feel like the despair couldn't get any deeper, the gods always organized help in some coincidental way. A friend I hadn't heard from in months or years would unexpectedly call and give me the key to whatever problem I was trying to solve. That kind of thing happened repeatedly.

I had read that we already know everything there is to know in the universe on some spiritual level but we've forgotten how to access this information. The answers that came by apparent coincidence *were* leading me slowly back to health, even though I didn't pray to any god in particular.

I couldn't be a Christian because I knew too much about the political forces that had created its dogmas. Besides, my gut told me that god was inside me. I couldn't relate to the notion of god being some father figure out in the ether that may decide to help me if I just had enough faith. I was too much of a do-it-yourselfer for that.

No, it was clear that whether I was consciously trying to or not, I was developing a spiritual self. So if this spiritual self was somehow all-knowing, its name could only be Sofie, which means wisdom. Besides, I loved Meryl Streep, and I thought *Sophie's Choice* was a really great movie. I was learning the basic lessons of the movie—the redemptive powers of acceptance and love—over and over again through my own challenges.

So there we were: Fidelita, Tillie and Sofie. They kept me distracted and amused through some very rough times. If you saw me smiling even at my worst, Tillie was having a good day, I'd managed to stay out of Fidelita's torture chambers, or the gods had seen Sofie safely through another long, dark tunnel and out into the light again.

YA GOTTA LAUGH

Negative thinking clogs up the brain, and there
is no room for love and joy to flow in its free and
open way. Laughter cannot flow if it is not allowed
to be free and foolish.

Louise Hay

In the 1950s, Dow Chemical used the advertising tag
line "Better living through chemistry." It became
part of the English idiom. In the early '60s, Rachel
Carson's famous book *Silent Spring* detailed the hazards
posed to the environment and life itself by living through
chemicals. I always thought she made a good point. Then
I developed my own silent spring.

My escalating fatigue levels were the first sign that I
was becoming chronically ill. Then I lost forty pounds in
just two months. This I didn't mind. I'd tried for years to
lose weight without success. Now I could buy a new size
8 wardrobe; this was the good news. But I also became
acutely sensitive to airborne pollutants of all kinds.
Scented fabric softener. Women's perfume. Moulds.
Diesel exhaust fumes. Household cleaning products.

Almost all chemical smells affected my ability to move or think normally.

My outings began to require advance planning to minimize chemical exposure. Other habits had to change too. Household cleaners had to pass a "distant sniff test" before I could even consider buying them. I couldn't leave my bedroom window open in case my neighbour ran her dryer which vented just opposite. She always used "rain-scented" fabric softener and declined my requests to stop using this product. She said something about her (cancer-ridden) husband liking his clothes soft. *How ironic that it's rain-scented*, I thought. *Just leave your windows open and you'll get the real thing.* But such is the power of advertising that leads us to pay money for toxic fakes. I just wish she didn't have to inflict her choices on me.

Even with the best planning, I couldn't be sure I'd be able to walk from my car to the front door, a distance of about one hundred steps, because if I encountered someone wearing a strong perfume or stayed out just a little too long, my legs would refuse to keep me upright. More than once, I had to wait for someone to walk by on the street and call out for assistance. I lived on a quiet street in a very quiet neighbourhood, and the wait varied from two to twenty minutes. I've always had a stubborn streak that usually works in my favour. But when weeks went by and there was no sign of improvement, I knew I'd have to give in and stop driving.

I got the paperwork in place to use the disabled transit system, called HandyDART. My doctor, the officially authorized knower regarding my health, had to sign the forms. She gave an official label to my symptoms and described my encroaching disabilities, but she had no explanation for them, for why my chemical sensitivity appeared or why it kept getting worse.

Using HandyDART meant I had to become super organized. Trip bookings had to be made several days in advance, and if I forgot to book on the right day, I either couldn't get a ride or the time I needed. I'd have to go early and wait or pay for a taxi myself. A special bus comes right to my door at the prebooked time. HandyDART can be late, but I cannot, as the driver will only wait five minutes past the designated pickup time and then leave me behind if I'm not ready. Having always been a last-minute organizer, I had to become the model of advance preparation.

I appreciated the drivers escorting me to the bus and back to my door when I got home. No matter how tired I was or what nasty chemical I had encountered, I knew I'd always get to my house safely. No more waiting for passersby. I got door-to-door service for the same price as regular bus fare.

I began using a scooter to "walk" along the beach. This became my new favourite pastime. I loved walking in the forest park at the end of my street, but my favourite trails were barred by gates to try to exclude mountain bikers. The trails without gates made for an uncomfortably bumpy outing, so I settled happily for the beach. I knew I would soon have to use a wheelchair in the house as well. "Wall walking" just wasn't safe anymore, especially since my husband was out of town and I was alone in the house about fifty percent of the time.

Because I had the notion that I didn't want my legs to "forget" how to walk when I did have to use a wheelchair in the house, I started going to the swimming pool three times a week. I could still walk in the shallow water if I held on to the concrete edge. I made a standing booking with HandyDART for this, and a bus appeared at my door at 9:30 a.m. on Monday, Wednesday and Friday, and brought me home at 1:00 p.m. unless I cancelled in advance. It added discipline to my exercise program.

I got to know a lot of different drivers, and, by and large, they were an interesting lot. And they seemed to appreciate me too. Many of them told me my lively intellect and conversation made a pleasant change. When I shared rides, I found out what they meant. I learned more than I ever needed to know about stomach ulcers, backaches, heart problems and a host of other health challenges. The mostly elderly passengers complained with relish about their ailments, their doctors and the many drugs they were told to take. Most of which didn't really help them, they said. *Other than to give you a topic for conversation,* I'd think to myself. *And even if they rarely got much response.*

There were several drivers who moonlighted as musicians. One was a dragon boat racer who travelled to competitions around the world. Another was an artist and a refugee from the war in Bosnia. Whatever their backgrounds, I usually enjoyed my interactions with the drivers.

The year after HandyDART switched from gasoline- and propane-fuelled vehicles to diesel-fuelled ones, I met a driver named Hamish. I was still highly chemically sensitive, especially to the emissions in diesel exhaust.

These had a number of unpleasant effects on me, none of them immediately visible. Drivers just had to take my word about the problems they caused, and usually they did. If I had to breathe the diesel fumes for some reason, my head immediately started to ache, my hands became more numb and tingly, and even my sitting balance became disoriented. When I had to move, my co-ordination was affected.

I was told the HandyDART maintenance manager directed the drivers to leave the engines continuously running, even when they were loading passengers with the hoist directly in the exhaust outflow. Something about wearing out the engine parts faster if they had to be continually turned off and restarted. Given my reactions to the diesel exhaust, I requested that a memo be placed on my file directing that my ride's engine be turned off whenever I was entering and exiting the vehicle. HandyDART agreed and was supposed to tell every driver it sent out for me. If I was on a run sheet— that is, I was picked up by the same driver for the same ride on an ongoing basis—a notation was supposed to appear on the driver's passenger list. Often, though, I had to give the driver a gentle reminder. Until Hamish, they always responded well to my request.

My first encounter with Hamish was after a Friday session at the pool. I arrived in the lobby as usual a few minutes before my pickup time. I looked out the window and didn't see the HandyDART bus. I waited inside in the air conditioning, as it was a hot summer day. About ten minutes later, another pool patron told me my bus was outside. I went out to find a bus forward of where they normally parked. The vehicle's back door was open, and its diesel engine was running. A portly, white-haired driver appeared to be less than pleased with me. We had never met before, and it was now two minutes past my designated pickup time.

"I've been waiting for you for half an hour," he said with a scowl.

"I've been waiting inside for you," I said. "I couldn't see you from the window."

I didn't mention that my pickup time had only just passed, no matter how long he had been waiting, or that he should have come inside for me.

The driver left the engine running and started for the lift at the back of the vehicle.

"Excuse me," I said. "Could you please turn off the engine for me?"

"No," the driver replied. "My lift won't work if the engine isn't running."

"Are you sure?" I asked. "It usually works for other drivers with the engine off."

"Just get here and get in the bus," Hamish said.

"I'm sorry, but I can't."

"Why not?"

"Because I will be sick all afternoon from breathing the diesel fumes."

I had stayed well back and there was a good breeze. That answer was obviously not good enough for him.

"Just get on the lift," he commanded.

"I'm sorry, but I can't until I don't have to breathe the diesel fumes," I said. "There should be a note to that effect on my file. Maybe you could call dispatch and confirm this."

"I'm not calling dispatch. Just get on."

I thought about my out-of-country guests who would have arrived by now and be waiting at my home for me. They were only staying for the weekend, and the last thing I wanted was to greet them with a throbbing head and needing to lie down. My patience with this driver's intransigence passed its limit.

"Well, I'm not going to make myself sick breathing your exhaust, so if you refuse to turn your engine off for me you can just fuck off out of here. I'll make my own way home."

"Fine," the driver said. "And by the way, my name's Hamish."

I already knew his origin because of his Glaswegian accent. My sister had been married to another Glaswegian. Funny, I hadn't gotten along with him either.

I cut my losses and called a taxi. Half an hour later, I was home feeling as well as it was possible for me to feel at that point in my life.

I thoroughly enjoyed the weekend with my guests. I told them and my husband about the altercation with Hamish but then put it out of my mind. I couldn't help thinking when I went back to the pool the next week, though, whether Hamish would be back on Friday. I called to find out if that would be the case. Although the reservation agent couldn't definitely confirm that Hamish would be my driver, she told me I was on a standing booking and it looked like nothing had changed over the past week. She said she was not allowed to change my driver when I asked if she would.

The butterflies in my stomach kept getting bigger and more active the closer it got to Friday at one o'clock. I decided I really didn't need the aggravation, cancelled the ride and took a taxi home again. I'd solved the problem for another week, but I knew I couldn't afford to do this every Friday. I kept praying that HandyDART would just put me on a different bus. After all, schedules were rearranged for internal reasons all the time. I called in again, and again was told that nothing had changed. I decided I'd have to steel myself to encountering Hamish again.

On the next Friday, there he was, waiting in view of the door this time. *Well, maybe things won't be so bad after all*, I thought hopefully.

Hamish escorted me to a bus parked in the alley. With its engine turned off. On the lift, I asked if there would be any additional passengers.

"Why?" Hamish wanted to know.

"Well, I feel safest if I transfer into a seat, and if there are no other wheelchair passengers, it is easiest for me to transfer if I park in the middle instead of on the side."

Hamish didn't reply except to indicate that I should park on the far side of the bus away from the seat access.

"Are there other passengers?" I asked again.

"No," he said impatiently. "But I can't tie your scooter down in the middle."

Maybe it was my own stubborn streak that made me do it, or maybe it was my repugnance at the thought of having to take Hamish's arm and experience the reek of his pomade. Whatever the reason, I parked in the middle, saying that other drivers just moved the tie-down straps. I stood and transferred into the seat without Hamish's help. He backed my scooter up and drove it to the far side of the van from the seat access. Not very carefully either. He tied it down, and we drove to my home in silence.

Hamish had never been there before, and made the incorrect assumption that he should drop me off at my back gate. As we turned into the lane, I said, "I need to get off at the front. The back gate is locked and there are stairs going in this way anyhow." Hamish made no reply, but drove to the front of my house. I asked him to turn off the engine as he was getting out, but he pretended not to hear and just left the engine running.

It was clear he was being deliberately difficult. The lifts always go down with no power on, even if all the batteries are dead. When my scooter was untied, still on the far side of the van, I stood and moved awkwardly to it, holding on to the back of the seat. I refused Hamish's arm and fell into my scooter seat as soon as I could. I knew it would be less stressful if I held my tongue, but the comment just seemed to slip out.

"I thought HandyDART drivers were here to help those who can't help themselves. You seem to get some kind of perverse pleasure from being unhelpful."

"Just because you're sick, you don't need to get all bitter and twisted and take it out on others," he said. "Just get a life! There's nothing in those diesel fumes that'll hurt you. If you just tried being nice, you'd probably feel better."

Furious now, I decided not to respond. I headed for my front door. My husband opened it just in time to see me burst into tears. After hearing what had happened, he insisted on calling the HandyDART manager and demand I be removed from Hamish's run sheet. The manager had never deigned to respond to phone calls about any of my previous problems, so I held little hope for help from that quarter. To my surprise, the manager called Michael back. *Must be a guy-to-guy thing*, I thought. The manager promised to "investigate and advise."

The manager eventually advised that Hamish had put in a complaint about me because I told him to fuck off. He made no mention of any other aspect of our encounter. The manager confirmed there was a memo on my file about my sensitivity to diesel fumes, and that Hamish should have adhered to it. He said he could not bend the rules to move my ride to another driver's run sheet. However, he said that a written notice would be placed in Hamish's record of employment and that Hamish could be terminated after three of them. *"Could" is the operative term here*, I thought. *Given his attitude, there's no way I'm the first person to have complained about him.*

As my next potential meeting with Hamish approached, I called HandyDART again to check if I was still on his run sheet. The voice on the other end of the phone line was friendly and sympathetic when she heard the nature of the request.

"What's he done this time?" she said. "He's always giving people a hard time. But then others have written letters of commendation about the good service he's given."

To my great relief, the booking agent confirmed that my trip had been assigned to another driver. With only a small pang of self-censure, I thought, *Hamish probably wrote those letters himself or extorted a signature. The stench of his pomade alone would be enough to make me sign if he wouldn't let me out. Never mind the diesel.*

I encountered Hamish only once more when he came to pick me up from home some weeks later. Again, he left his engine running while he waited in front of my house until my pickup time. I caught the first whiff of the diesel even before I opened the front door. I didn't see it was Hamish until I got out to the street. Again, he had waited in his van instead of announcing his arrival by coming to the door. I didn't hesitate.

"I'm not riding with you. Please leave."

I made the mistake of calling for a taxi before I called HandyDART to advise that I would still want my ride coming home.

"Too late," I was told. "It's already cancelled."

The extra cab fare was a small price to pay to avoid the diesel fumes and the pomade.

Hamish retired about a year later. Every driver who heard of my adventures with Hamish told me about his retirement. The drivers usually started the story by announcing that they had some good news for me. Many of them, it seemed, had also had some kind of unpleasant run-in with him.

I could smile now. *Ya gotta laugh*, I thought. *Otherwise you'll cry. And life's too short for that.*

DEPP ON THE 911 LINE

> We treat people in terms of the categories into which they are placed rather than in (terms of) the fullness of their humanity.
>
> Frank Tannenbaum

Things were not good with my health. Rest was always the best medicine, but I was easily bored and had trouble just resting. So I compromised. I laid on the couch watching movies on video most afternoons. This still took some energy. But at least I wasn't cursing my fatigue, brain fog and the choices I'd made that put me in this predicament.

Instead, my attention was on the film stars' performances or the scripts. I was particularly partial to films starring Johnny Depp. He struck me as an old soul, and the depth of feeling in his eyes always went straight to my heart. Although not handsome, he had his own magnetism.

Wouldn't you know it, my health setback occurred just after I signed up for a night school class to develop ideas for the novel I'd been kicking around in my mind for some time. I prayed I would somehow find the creativity and energy to write my assignments each week and that I wouldn't feel too embarrassed when I read them to the class. The theme of my novel had to do with the cultural shaming of sexual identity. I knew I was a good academic writer, and fast, as long as I had an immediate deadline to motivate me. I hoped these qualities would help me through the course.

It was Wednesday night about 5:30. I was home alone. My writing class started at 7:00, and the HandyDART bus was scheduled to pick me up at 6:30. I was resting on the couch, trying to clear my head. I'd be asked to read my work in class for the first time that night, and I was still feeling brain-fogged despite the rest. But I had to be ready when the bus arrived at my door. They could be late, but I couldn't.

I sat up to try my usual technique, which was 60% upper body strength, 20% leg strength and 20% sheer determination. This usually got me up off the couch into a standing position from which I could pivot and sit in my wheelchair just in front of me. It didn't work as it normally did. The occupational therapists had suggested several times that I raise the couch, a restored 1930s edition with show wood and interesting detailing which was particularly low. I'd had the restoration done at a time when I was stronger than now. With Michael home, it didn't matter. He could easily swing my 115-pound frame into the wheelchair when lifting it myself was too much for me.

But he wasn't home now. I tried again to stand up. Same story. I was hot, so I took off my top clothes to try to cool down, hoping this would help. Michael called. He was close to home, thirty minutes drive when the traffic was light. I didn't tell him about my predicament, but I asked if he planned to make any stops along the way.

"No," he said.

"Good," I said, "then I'll see you before I have to leave at 6:30."

I returned to my efforts to stand up, taking particular care with my foot and hand placements to get the most lift out of my limited strength. I was starting to feel the need to pee. One of the features of my health problems was the typically short lead time between my bladder's notification of its need and its actual voiding. I tried to stand up again. And again. And again.

Traffic would probably be heavy at this time of night, so I knew I couldn't rely on Michael arriving in time to help me get up. I also knew there was no way I was going to allow my bladder to void on my cherished restored couch.

Why didn't I just tell Michael I was having trouble when he called? I dialled his cell number to find out if he would be home soon. It was six o'clock, and his voicemail invited me to leave a message. Not the response I wanted. I wondered if he had stopped after all. I put some top clothes back on. The need to void my bladder was getting urgent now, but one last mighty heave didn't give the desired result.

I could think of no alternative now but to slide off the couch and try to scoot myself off the carpet and onto the hardwood. If I had the strength, I'd try for the linoleum. I made it to the hardwood. Now I had two problems: I still had to get up, and I'd have to change my clothes. I'd need help for both if I was going to make it to the class.

I dialled a neighbour's phone number and left a message in case they were home and just screening their calls. I then prioritized my other neighbours to call as I got their numbers from Directory Assistance. One after another answered with a machine.

It was 6:15 p.m.

I started to sob, letting out my pent-up frustration. The floor felt hard and cold. If I was to have any chance of making my class, I had one option left. I dialled 911. The operator was unable to understand me through my tears, so I hung up and tried to bring my voice under control. Then I dialled again. Still lots of tears, but I got a different, more patient operator. It took a while to assure the operator that I wasn't hurt, I just needed a lift. The operator took my address.

"They're on their way," she said.

I was curled into the fetal position with my upper body on the carpet. My lower body, now sodden, had made it to the hardwood. I waited, trying to stop sobbing. I heard footsteps approaching the back of the house and saw Michael through the window. He apparently didn't see me. He left and returned a minute later with another load of luggage. When Michael did see me on the floor, he rushed in and put his arms around me.

"What happened?" he asked.

The fire and rescue team arrived at the front door less than ten seconds later. Michael had just enough time to get a garbage bag on my wheelchair seat. Three tall, uniformed men filled the low-ceilinged space.

"Are you hurt?" one of the firemen asked.

"Just my pride," I replied.

"Well ma'am, we're here to help. That's our job. How is the best way to get you back in your chair?"

This from the youngest of the three. He was very tall, very handsome and had short black hair. Otherwise he looked just like Johnny Depp. *He's got the eyes. Just give him a long brown ponytail, and he's a ringer*, I thought.

Michael wheeled the chair up behind me. The black-haired Johnny Depp put his arms under mine, lifted, and I was in the chair.

I smiled through my tears.

"Thank you," I said.

"Don't ever hesitate to call. This is what we're here for," he reiterated. "What happened? Did you fall?"

The whole story came out. The rescue team was kindness and discretion personified. No embarrassment. Just matter-of-factness. They stayed a few minutes to make sure I was okay. Johnny asked if there was anything else they could do. By this time my sense of humour had returned.

"How are you at cooking dinner?"

Johnny smiled and said, "Sorry I asked."

His colleague joined in my spirit, "You picked the right guy. He's the best cook at the station," he said.

Later, I smiled to myself as I thought, *I should've looked to see if Johnny's name or number was on his uniform. Then if he was on shift, I'd be in need of rescue.*

It was 6:30 p.m. Fortunately, HandyDART had to send a disabled taxi, which was late. With Michael's help,

I washed, put on clean clothes and got my bag in the scooter. The taxi arrived at my door at 6:50 p.m.

"They sent me to the wrong street, ten blocks over. Our dispatcher had to check with HandyDART," the driver said.

I smiled. "No problem," I replied. *God is watching me,* I thought.

I got to my classroom just as the instructor was starting her lecture for the evening. Twenty minutes later, I was reading the opening of my novel that describes a young boy's sexual awakening. The class sat in silence for several long moments after I stopped.

Finally one of my classmates said, "This is powerful stuff."

If you didn't know I was sobbing on the floor in a puddle of urine just an hour and a half ago, I thought, *you'd think I was perfectly normal. But then Jonny Depp wouldn't have come to rescue me. I wonder if I can work this into my writing somehow.*

GENES AND BELIEF

During times of universal deceit, telling the truth becomes a revolutionary act.

George Orwell

I grew up on a farm in a conservative Mennonite community. Higher education was not encouraged— especially for girls—so I was in my thirties before I went to university. I analyzed my family's religious belief system for an anthropology course paper. I built on scholarly literature about the emphasis some cultures apply to maintaining tradition and opposing change. It's always seemed to me that science is a bit like this. Of course, scientists say their work is about creating new knowledge which creates change, but I'm not convinced this is always true.

At university I was intrigued by the views of the world I discovered in my social science classes. I'll never forget reading how the knowledge we take for granted is created through political processes—and always serves someone's purpose. I was impressed with Thomas Kuhn's idea of "normal" science—science shaped by a pre-existing paradigm. Kuhn said that the goal of normal science is to confirm its paradigm, not to change it. He said scientific "revolutions" only happen when enough scientists buy into new explanations for results that don't fit the dominant paradigm. He also wrote that science has shown itself to be fully susceptible to "fad, fashion, delusion, and prejudice."

The acceptance of Einstein's quantum theories in physics is usually used to illustrate Kuhn's work on paradigm shifts. Einstein is given star billing as "the one" who brought about the scientific revolution from the old Newtonian, mechanical view of the world. But Einstein's conclusions were foreshadowed by many other scientists for nearly half a century.

I also studied the ways that funding and media attention help keep science consistent with tradition rather than with the romantic notion of opening new frontiers. I've often annoyed friends by talking about how what passes as a new frontier is really just "normal" science. For me, the current fad for genetic research is "normal" science consistent with a long outdated Newtonian paradigm of medicine.

These ideas were only strengthened when I began my research on MS, the label medical doctors use to describe the health challenges that put me in a wheelchair within two years. The public voice of health problems like mine, the MS Society, is heavily committed to genetic and other "normal" scientific research. Despite regular pronouncements claiming advances through the research it funds, after more than fifty years they still say MS has no known cause and no known cure. The society has recently expanded its services to include young children who are diagnosed with MS. Until a few years ago MS was only seen in adults, so I have to conclude that research is not looking in the right places.

Although I won't give money for research, I will give the MS Society time by writing numerous articles on "alternative" medicine for their newsletters. The responses I get tell me that many people want to hedge their bets between alternative and conventional medical approaches to their health. This openness to alternative points of view also applies to the society's annual conferences in my province. The organizers present speakers from both conventional medical and holistic ways of thinking about health. I helped plan the first three such conferences.

The last one, almost accidentally, was opened by a scientist named Bruce Lipton, formerly a genetic researcher and medical school professor. Bruce now travels the speaker's circuit full time and describes his former life as a form of purgatory at best.

The planning committee had already chosen the speakers for a two-day annual conference when someone suggested Bruce. As committee chair, I was skeptical about revisiting decisions that had already been made, but I didn't want to cut off innovative new possibilities. So we committed to examining Bruce Lipton's website. There I found a twenty-six page list of academic research publications and a photo. While Bruce is a good looking man, his publication titles did nothing for me. Then my colleague circulated a two-hour lecture video. I was blown away. Bruce made a very complex message accessible, and as he later wrote to me, "There is great joy in the new science because it reveals how we can influence our lives."

Media messages about genetic research are designed to convey the ideas of progress and hope. We have to wait for the "experts" to make the progress (i.e., to do more research) after which we'll hear what new drug we have to take to be rid of our health problems. Until then, we just have to manage as best we can on hope. Until I met Bruce, hope didn't seem like enough.

According to him, genetic research is showing a larger role for environment and belief than for genes. Bruce speaks of how genetic science indicates only a "blueprint" role for genes, and how such results had been accumulating for fifteen years. He says cells will continue to live without their genes, but it's only when they need to repair a worn out part that they can't because the "blueprint" is gone. He says that the health of a cell does not depend on its genes in most cases, and that accumulating research shows environment and belief are more important. If this is true, it's a whole new ball game—or paradigm. Even a scientific revolution.

Television newscasts give me a different message. They suggest the secrets of life itself are being revealed by the latest discoveries in genetic research. I guess the idea that I have to believe I can be well first and then look hard at my environment for causes of my health problems doesn't make good news copy. But it does illustrate what Bruce means when he says that the new science shows that I can influence my own health without waiting for direction from the "experts."

My case depends on my environment and how I've reacted to it. It's unique to me, and I'll be the most important factor in my recovery. And recovery is possible. I always believed this, even though I had to keep it to myself to avoid having others treat me like I was not very well informed or crazy. Or both.

I felt awe and joy as I started to understand the implications of the new science as Bruce described them. I feel the same way in the shadows of the forest floor when a single dust-speckled shaft of sunlight suddenly beams across my path through a thick canopy of branches to highlight a single fern frond, a spider's web or a few vine maple leaves. Seeing this fleeting light and the natural beauty it accentuates always leaves me with a sense of magic and occasion.

Other members of the conference planning committee felt the same way I did, so we unanimously decided to reorganize our slate of speakers and invite Bruce to open the event.

When he spoke months later, I sat at a table against the back wall of the conference room. I was a little nervous about the complexity of his message and how it would be received by our audience. The audience was transfixed by Bruce's torrents of words, their implications illustrated by the movements of bits of coloured, bendable plastic pipe in his hands. Although Bruce spoke for almost two hours without breaks or questions, the audience of hundreds sat in raptured silence until he was finished. Then a thunderous burst of applause went on for several minutes, and those who could, stood and gave him an ovation like I had never seen at these conferences before.

Lunch was served to the rest of us, but Bruce had a line-up of people wanting to talk with him. The line-up was still there and had to be moved to make way for our afternoon speakers.

The first event of the afternoon was a panel of four people telling their own stories of recovery from the "incurable" problems called MS. Each one had followed a different but holistic path. They provided powerful personal confirmations to Bruce's evidence of the importance of belief and environment to overcoming even the most challenging health problems.

I had hoped to be able to tell my own recovery story, but it was not to be. I actually felt worse for some months after the conference, which severely taxed my capacity to believe in the possibility of recovery. But I found it was true that I had to look harder at my environment for answers, and that I had more layers to work through than I'd thought. I was learning a lot, but I have to admit there were times when the pain made it hard to even think of walking again.

I turned fifty a few months after I met Bruce. I was still in a tunnel of pain and disability where the light of recovery was just a dim belief at some unseen end. I'd been dreading this birthday for months. It made me feel old, and it fed fears that I was beyond the age of recovery. It didn't help when a friend shared her disquiet about my belief in recovery, saying she had only ever seen me getting worse and felt my optimism was misguided.

Then a television interview with a famous Hollywood producer I heard by chance renewed my beliefs. I had never been interested in seeing his movies as they struck

BARBARA ALLDRITT

me as the worst kind of Hollywood rewriting of history. These films made millions of dollars at the box office, however, and were obviously popular with many people. The producer spoke enthusiastically about how every sector of the population loved his films. Then he hesitated and seemed to have a second thought before correcting himself, saying "The only demographic that doesn't is older women."

Hearing this, I suddenly felt good about being fifty. It seems that older women, the group I hadn't wanted to join, usually see the world a little differently to the majority. They prefer a more genuine picture where hope and happy endings are real, not just celluloid fantasies.

A few months later, I received a compendium of MS research results from a friend, another "older woman." It included a study describing how self-efficacy, defined as the belief that one can competently cope with a challenging situation, is a very good predictor of improvements in health. It was more proof of the importance of belief just when I needed it most.

Others may think I'm living in a fantasy to believe that I'll recover my health and walk again, but I'm ready to face my mortality either walking or wheeling. Having met Bruce Lipton, I choose to believe his version of the causes of health problems instead of the news stories touting the latest genetic research pronouncements.

My unconventional beliefs fit my status as an older woman, and the "abnormal" science confirms their rationality. I'm sure I'm looking in the right paradigm for answers—they're somewhere in my beliefs and my environment, not in my genes. I can do something about this. The future I believe in will come even if—maybe especially because—I'm an older woman. These thoughts keep me smiling. I can accept smile wrinkles whether they come from my "blueprint" or my beliefs and environment.

MY GARDEN COCOON

Happiness is a journey, not a destination. For a long time it seemed to me that life was about to begin— real life. But there was always some obstacle in the way, something to be gotten through first, some unfinished business, time still to be served, a debt to be paid. At last it dawned on me that these obstacles were my life. This perspective has helped me to see there is no way to happiness. Happiness is the way. So treasure every moment you have and remember that time waits for no one.

Alfred D. Souza

F aith Popcorn, a reputed futurist, author and CEO, coined the catchy term "cocooning" to describe the baby boomer generation's shift of priorities from work and activism to home and family. This focus on the home, on creating a "cocoon," Popcorn predicted, would make gardening a hot interest. I never set out to prove her right, but the lure of a connection to the beauty of nature right outside my front door became irresistible.

My tiny hundred-year-old cottage boasted a ragged front garden with large trees and a hedge, but no grass. I had been perfectly happy to let it be colonized by a weed with pretty blue flowers while I worked, but my chronic illness that put me in a wheelchair gave me a lot more time at home.

I began visualizing what my garden could look like without the weeds, overgrown laurels and stumps of trees long gone to the landfill. There was a patinated moss-covered Japanese stone lantern in the garden when we bought the property. The lantern reminded me of the temple gardens we'd seen on a visit to Japan and inspired me to research the essential elements of balance and beauty in a Japanese garden. I was intrigued with the ways they allow one element to represent another, and these thoughts led me to dream of creating a river of rocks flowing across my garden.

I'd need a detailed plan so I could direct someone with good balance and strong legs to execute my ideas since I couldn't realize them alone while in a wheelchair. I dreamed for three years before I had the full picture and the right help.

First I asked Michael to do the work. He is an engineer, and as is the habit of many engineers, tends to think in straight lines. He laid out a river course that looked like a canal to me despite my insistence that rivers meander. After that, we were happy to hire someone who was willing to follow my meandering directions.

First I hired a friend's twenty-something son, but his all-night partying interfered with his desire to get up in the morning. Now I had straight lines of rocks, gaping holes from the stumps our friend's son dug out *and* weeds in my garden. Not really an improvement! And the winter rains were on their way.

The next spring, I found the right person, Nova, a Yugoslavian refugee artist. He possessed the perfect combination of an artistic sensibility, a strong work ethic, a knowledge of power tools and a love of nature. It didn't hurt that he was tall and handsome too. Michael was only too happy to have Nova do the work while he spent the month of May in Europe.

Nova prepared the space over the first weekend, which mostly involved digging out the parasitic bluebells that had taken over. He used a pickaxe to dig down the six to eight inches to reach the plants' bulbs. If we didn't get the bulbs out, he said, the plants would just keep coming back. Inch by inch, Nova dug the space with amazingly good humour. It helped that the sun was shining. And we told one another our favourite jokes, even though our language differences necessitated a lot of explanations.

Nova filled numerous garbage bags with weeds and other debris. He dug out the last of the old stumps and filled in all the holes. On Nova's smoke breaks, I got to know him and received a few glimpses into what living in a war zone was like.

"People think is so terrible. But is ordinary," Nova said.

Nova told me that the destruction of all that used to be familiar in time itself becomes familiar. He said he got used to starting a generator for electric power and only using it for short periods a few times a day. He got used to the constant hunger and search for food. You could get blasé about the sound of missiles whining overhead, he said, and only run for cover in the last seconds before they land. I valued these insights and the bond our work was creating as much as I did my clean garden space.

The next step was to create a new outline of a meandering river. Nova needed no direction in this. Our thoughts harmonized. We were going to need a lot more large shore rocks to complete the job, but I thought I had that challenge figured out. We also needed a large quantity of small stones representing the water, so Nova picked up bags of pebbles from a landscape supplier every morning for a week before starting his day job.

A friend came up from Seattle for the long weekend, and we shifted our attention to the garden's centrepiece. Our first task was to create more visibility for the Japanese lantern by placing it on top of a large, flat stone I had collected from a neighbourhood construction site. The half-ton stone would have to be moved then Nova would drill a hole through its twelve-inch thickness and thread electric wiring up for the lantern's light bulb.

I rented a power drill with a fifteen-inch masonry bit. The rental store staff warned me that rock is usually harder than concrete, for which the bit was designed, so if the bit broke, I would have to pay an extra hundred dollars to replace it. I was in the shower when I heard the rattle of the drill start up. I closed my eyes and prayed. The drilling seemed to go on for a very long time, but by the time I was dressed, had finished breakfast and gone outside, the drill and its intact bit had already been returned to the rental store.

Nova centred the rock over the top of the electrical conduit coming out of the ground. He then threaded the electric wire up through the newly-drilled hole, and connecting it into the lantern was almost complete. In a few minutes, I flicked the switch in the porch and the lantern lit up. My garden centrepiece was everything I hoped it would be! The occasion deserved champagne, but we had too much work still to do.

Another friend delivered a trailer load of shore-sized rocks collected from a nearby riverbank. I hoped I could persuade him to bring all I needed, but one load was his limit. And this turned out to be twenty percent of my needs, at best. I decided to rent a truck for Nova to collect the rest later.

My friend from Seattle took me shopping for plants while Nova did a late afternoon overtime shift at his day job. Having researched the plants that would do well in the shade of my north-facing, tree-surrounded site, I bought ornamental grasses, a low, spreading juniper, hostas and a Japanese aralia, among others. But when I had my selections home, I knew I would need as many plants again to achieve the lushness I wanted.

Nova came up with the idea of recreating the appearance of a riverbank on one side of our stone river. The land sloped downwards there, and building up a bank would mean I'd need fewer plants to fill the space. We could create interest with tree roots and stones in the bank face, and we had plenty of soil!

We decided this around seven in the evening, and Nova and I immediately went to the beach twenty-odd blocks away to look for driftwood roots for our planned riverbank. I drove down on my scooter, Nova in the car. The plan was for Nova to check the forest above while I reconnoitered the beach below from an adjacent path. We would communicate any finds by cell phone.

We found only one root small enough to fit in the trunk of the car, so we loaded it. The rest were beautiful, but huge—forest-sized when I needed dwarf-sized. Nova said we needed a gas chainsaw to cut small chunks off the big trunks, but I only owned an electric chainsaw which would do us no good at the beach.

I was in luck as I had a neighbour who was willing to lend us his gas chainsaw. Nova took it to the beach early Saturday morning. He came back hours later with no wood, looking very stressed. The starter pull cord dangled pathetically from the side of the saw. Nova thought it was wrecked and had gone to see how much a replacement would cost. He felt responsible for returning a functioning saw to my neighbour, and I assured him Michael would be able to fix the borrowed saw when he got home.

Nova threw himself into moving soil to clear the stress of the morning while I checked the price of chainsaw rentals and brainstormed other borrowing possibilities.

That evening, Nova studied the root we had, considering how to cut it. His suggestion was brilliant, but had nothing to do with our riverbank simulation. We had about ten large ferns waiting to be replanted in a grouping under some trees on the opposite side of the yard from the riverbank. Nova suggested he create a setting for the ferns by building up the soil and laying out gnarly pieces of driftwood to create the impression of a tree stump with exposed roots. By now, I knew my labour budget was well over my estimates, but I thought it was a great idea, so Nova wheeled in more soil.

The next evening I got home to find Nova busy creating the tree stump setting for the ferns. By the time he was ready to start planting, it was already nine o'clock at night and dark. We only had a few days left before Michael arrived home and I wanted to have the work finished by then, so we hung a halogen lamp on an overhanging tree branch and kept going.

Nova had had his hair cut earlier that day. It was very short, and he joked that it made him look like a Nazi. We had to cut a lot of the fern fronds out for transplanting, and we laughed about giving them Nazi haircuts too. It was 10:30 p.m. before they were all back in the soil. Nova drank a beer, and we admired his creation while we watered in the replanted ferns. It was a work of art—a living sculpture!

The next morning Nova took a rental truck to collect enough rocks to finish simulating our river's shores. I called another friend and asked if we could borrow his gas chainsaw. The answer was yes, but we'd have to pick it up from the saw's co-owner. It didn't seem like a problem.

Nova finally arrived with the rocks. We had only forty-five minutes before the rental truck was due back, and the return site was a thirty-minute drive away. The floor of the truck box was covered with hundreds of rocks. Nova was going to need help to unload them if I was to avoid a late return penalty on the truck rental. I buzzed up and down the street on my scooter. There was no one about, but one neighbour's door was ajar—the keenest gardener on the block. I called him, and he arrived with his gloves on a minute later. In ten minutes we had a satisfying pile of shore rocks on the side of the street. Nova had hand-picked each one for its smoothness and pleasing shape. The rental truck got back to the depot on time.

Nova started painting in our shore with beautiful, smoothed ovals of stone. I left him to it for a short visit with my brother, Fred, who was passing through Vancouver. Fred took me shopping for more plants. I was torn between budget concerns and wanting to fill my space with lush greenery, but I loaded the cart with most of what I wanted. As Fred put my plants onto the counter by the till, I got out my credit card, but he was faster than me. He insisted on paying for everything. Fred said I should think of him every time I looked out to the mountain fire shrubs on the riverbank. I accepted gratefully.

Nova had finished creating the river's shores while we were shopping and went to pick up the second borrowed gas chainsaw. Perhaps the concerns were legitimate, perhaps it was prejudice against Nova's eastern European accent, but the saw's co-owner declined to lend it to us. Another hit on my budget! I asked Nova to go and rent a saw to get the wood we needed from the beach.

He brought a number of small root pieces and a large curling chunk of water-smoothed yellow wood, probably cedar. He initially thought the large piece could help stabilize the riverbank, but as it waited for placement, its serpentine shape spoke to Nova. He placed it as a sculptural statement next to my garden's street entrance. It is perfect there!

Nova brought a little piece of his past along with the driftwood. He excitedly drew some wilting leaves from his breast pocket.

"Do you know what is these?" he asked.

"They look like prickly leaves to me," I said blankly.

"These are—how you call in English?—nettle leaves. We have only these and rice to eat every day in first year of war. I don't think they here in Canada. You use every part of nettle plant—is either food or medicine. I feel good I know is here too."

I felt honoured Nova had become so comfortable with me during our work together. When I first met him, he had been reluctant to speak much about the unfortunate circumstances that brought him to Canada as a refugee. His presence now made me feel safer. Nova, and me by association, could survive any disaster nature or government might visit on us with help from the lowly nettle plant.

It was clear Nova was getting very tired. Between his day job and creating my garden, he had been working sixteen hours a day for over three weeks. We still had the final planting to do, and Michael was arriving home later that evening. I told Nova we should stop and finish when he felt rested, but he insisted on finishing.

I watched from the deck and surveyed the changes of the last weeks. *In this tiny space*, I thought, *I have something for every mood.* There is a lot to look at. The Japanese aralia, now ensconced in my Chinese dragon pot, stood at the corner of the house. Nova surrounded the pot's base with rocks. A clay planter with flaming orange impatience plants enlivened the deck under the front room window.

An armandii clematis climbed up and over a lattice screen at the end of the deck, its white flowers giving off a rich early spring perfume. A wind chime in front of the lattice sang gently in the breeze. Brilliant orange, yellow, red and pink rose-like flowers of everbearing begonias brightened the shade in a raised wooden planter box that separated the deck from the garden. Yellow- and green-leafed periwinkle drooped over the planter wall, its blue flowers would herald the arrival of spring in coming years.

On the north and south edges of the east side of the plot, two branches of the rock river flowed toward the curving concrete footpath from the house to the street. The path is wider at the house than the street, creating an illusion of distance.

From the aralia across a path bordering the south arm of the rock river is a pitted lava rock with a bubbler fountain set in the top water-worn depression. Water flows from hole to hole and then spills over the bottom of the rock to be collected in a hidden reservoir and pumped back up again. Michael created the fountain the previous year, and moss now colours it green, thriving in the damp. Nova gave it a new setting by flowing the "water" pebbles of our rock river around it.

The two branches of my river joined after they crossed the concrete footpath to the west side of the garden. A juniper marked the point. Graceful fountains of ornamental grass mounds lined the south shore of the joined river branches below the deck planter box. The riverbank Nova created is on the other shore. Dwarf purple irises bloomed in the "water's" edge. Lime-green leafed spirea, red-berried skimmia and flaming mountain fire shrubs to remind me of my brother sat atop the riverbank along with bleeding hearts and other woodland flowers. Bunchberry grows out from among the tree roots set in the riverbank.

A Zen five-rock placement Michael created is set between the riverbank and a large mauve-flowering rhododendron. A tall standing rock looks like a smiling garden angel to me after a little crack appeared on its face. A miniature version of the Australian Ayers Rock collected water on its top for birds and insects. A flat, heart-shaped rock almost touched the river shore. Irish moss would soon cover the soil among them. Astilbe and bush fuchsia lives happily in the shade behind the Zen rock placement.

The wood sculpture Nova collected at the beach stood between the rhododendron and a laurel hedge screening the garden from the street. A low growing plant with white flowers entwined with blue flowering companula set it off. Across the footpath next to the street was the north branch of the river. A large holly sheltered it, and a skimmia bloomed among the shore rocks underneath. Hostas and ivy drew my eye from the river to the profusion of ferns set in our newly created "old" tree stump.

My stone lantern stood proudly in front of the ferns, ivy already reaching up to colour its new rock base. The lantern frequently draws the eyes and compliments of passersby. More hostas thrived in the dappled shade on its south side. A tall, four-branched weeping birch was the backdrop for forest trilliums that flower white in spring, turn to pink then purple and finally to green as the summer progresses. The fountain the birds consider theirs bubbles beside them; it is rarely without a feathered visitor. All different kinds of birds bathe there, from the exotic hummingbirds and yellow warblers to the more mundane robins, juncos, stellar jays and even shy little wrens. I only hope the neighbourhood cats don't discover this paradise.

Michael arrived home as scheduled and walked slowly up the footpath, taking in the changes since he left. His eye went first to the riverbank.

"That's a great feature," he said. "Where did all the extra soil come from?"

I was pleased for Nova's sake. Engineers are trained to see potential problems, but I hoped Michael would see the beauty first and worry about soil slumping or some other engineering concern later. We told Michael my riverbank had resulted in his garden space in the back of the house becoming smoother and more even than it was when he left. He smiled and thanked us. Nova showed him how the height of the soil in the riverbank was supported with large rocks hidden in the back of it.

When Michael finished looking at his new front garden, I told him we had a job for him. The neighbour's gas chainsaw was on the deck, and I wanted Nova to be able to leave with no sense of unfinished business. As I had thought, Michael was able to fix it, clean it and oil it with Nova's help in twenty minutes. Nova returned it to my neighbour, who had no idea his saw came back to him in better condition than it left.

As Nova prepared to go home for a well-deserved rest, I reflected on the past intense weeks. I had bonded with a new friend. Nova created much more than I visualized over the previous three years. He gave me a detailed work of art in stone, driftwood and woodland plants.

I've experienced a metamorphosis along with my garden. When I consider whether I want to join the bustle at the beach, the tranquil beauty outside my door usually wins out. I rarely go to the beach on my scooter anymore and have become more meditative, less driven. Just sitting and resting by my garden now feels like "doing something." Noticing my trilliums dying back and thinking about interplanting them with fall blooming bulbs, or how trusting and beautiful the birds are that visit the fountain, or smiling back at my garden angel all count as "doing something."

My garden "cocoon" is painted with the art of nature, real and represented. It keeps me in touch with the movements and moods of the seasons. A butterfly has emerged!

FOR RICHER FOR POORER - ROCKEFELLER'S WORLD

> Ill fares the land, to hastening ills a prey,
> Where wealth accumulates, and men decay.
>
> *The Deserted Village* by Oliver Goldsmith

I sometimes wish people wouldn't give me things because then I wouldn't have to look after them or find places to keep them. The "black hole" in my attic is already full to capacity. I also sometimes wish I didn't know some of the things I know. That memory was like the attic that I'll clear out one day. Or like a child's Etch A Sketch, I could just give my head a shake and the sands of my memory would be smooth again, clear and ready for new memories to be sketched in. Less troubling memories. More joyous memories.

This wish came true when I published a story about how someone with a chronic and apparently incurable illness recovered his health. If he had accepted the doctors' prognosis, he would have started saving for a wheelchair. But he didn't. His recovery began when he started drinking a folk remedy he prepared himself, the fermented tea known as kombucha. Reaction to this story helped write new memories over some troubling knowledge about how Rockefeller interests work to shape the world we live in, and not always for the better. It was just like shaking the Etch A Sketch.

I was a university student when I first began to understand the global reach of the Rockefeller business empire. I researched and wrote about the so-called "Green Revolution," the misnamed movement that gave us the chemical agriculture that is the norm today, for an economic history class. Before that, every farm was organic; no certification was necessary. Petrochemical business interests, chief among them the Rockefellers', funded studies with the potential to expand their market for agricultural chemicals. A logical business plan, no doubt, with great PR possibilities in a world with a rapidly-increasing population. As for redistribution of the highly-concentrated ownership of land and food supplies so that the hungry could feed themselves, well, that would be "communist." Anything given that label was automatically off the agenda. No Western business or government would go there!

Studies in Mexico in the 1930s apparently demonstrated that fields using inputs of chemical fertilizers, pesticides and herbicides produced higher crop yields than untreated fields. These products, of course, are made from petrochemicals that increase the cost of food production and result in reduced soil nutrient content. From this start, food research institutes dedicated to expanding industrialized and chemicalized agriculture crept around the world, all conveniently justified by high population growth.

Sometimes government needed a little push, as not all of them welcomed the new agriculture without a fight. In the 1960s, India resisted this expensive Western model of industrial agriculture, knowing that its adoption would result in millions of farmers being forced off the land. Never afraid to play the bully, the United States told the Indian government that if they did not adopt "modern" agricultural practices, American aid dollars would no longer flow in their direction.

I spent most of the four years of my undergraduate studies amassing knowledge of this kind. Although it was profoundly depressing, I was hooked. I couldn't stop reading. I dealt with my depression by throwing myself into activism, and channelled it through the World University Service of Canada (WUSC). I helped organize film festivals and other awareness-raising events. At Christmas we sold crafts made by Third World artisans working with WUSC to develop business and marketing skills.

The First World-Third World dinners we organized were my favourite activity, though, and the most lucrative. These dinners were an experiential simulation of global inequities. A random draw at the door sent 20% of curious attendees to First World tables set with china, crystal wine glasses and white tablecloths. Well-dressed servers waited on them, their glasses topped up after every sip. They were served a four-course meal with steak. The other 80% went to tables representing Asia, Africa or South America. No tablecloths or wine glasses there.

They got chipped bowls and bent spoons. They had to help themselves from large pots filled with enough food for about half the table. Carbohydrates only, no protein. "Beggars" circulated with empty bowls, and sometimes fights broke out. After the dinner had made its point, there was a band, dancing, a cash bar and healthy profits from junk food sales.

Some years later as a graduate student, I read a book by a historian about how the Rockefellers had bought into the pharmaceutical industry in the early twentieth century. The academic writing and detailed documentation were as effective a cure for insomnia as any sleeping pill. The upshot was not surprising to me given what I already knew about the Green Revolution. After buying into pharmaceuticals, they commissioned Abram Flexner to prepare a report on the "future of medicine." Not surprisingly, Flexner concluded that the future of medicine was in pharmaceutical drugs and university-trained medical doctors.

Rockefeller began giving millions of dollars to university medical schools, and the curriculum shifted to reflect pharmaceutical perspectives. In the 1920s, university-trained medical doctors had been organizing and lobbying for more income, a greater share of business and higher social status for at least a hundred years without much success. So the Flexner report suited them too.

At that time most doctors' treatments were harsh and as likely to do harm as good, whereas the most helpful and popular people in times of need were traditional herbalists, homeopaths and others whose knowledge came from perspectives we would now call "alternative."

The American Congress adopted the Flexner report and declared all manner of health care practitioners illegal or, at best, suspect. This was when midwifery was outlawed in the United States and Canada probably because they provided too much competition for university-trained medical doctors.

Now almost no one remembers that the first Canadian hospital used only homeopathic treatments. Today, modern North American medicine is focused on pharmaceutical drugs and surgery. I was depressed for ten years about this and other knowledge of how skewed modern life had become to the benefit of large financial interests in the global economy. Then I became chronically fatigued and had to stop working. I didn't have to think about these larger problems anymore because I was too busy trying to become well again myself, but I avoided pharmaceutical drugs in the process.

It felt like a hot bullet passing through my consciousness when I read about Rockefeller interests funding yet another attempt to manage our perceptions. Just a few short lines in the editorial of an alternative magazine told how he and allied interests had paid for a group, chaired by a well-known public figure, to develop a global economic plan good for business and a way of selling such a plan to the public. The editorial was written in response to the devastating impacts of my provincial government's application of this plan, but the standard elements are familiar in governments around the world. Reduce spending on the social needs of citizens while making it easier for business interests to control the earth's natural resources and increase and keep profits.

Health, jobs and the environment, not to mention the poor, don't figure in this equation except for the usual political promises that are not kept.

But back to kombucha. My article about this folk remedy had just come out when the third Rockefeller incursion into my consciousness occurred. Kombucha contains interferons, which are used in treating cancer. Ronald Reagan is said to have used kombucha against prostate cancer. Russian dissident physicist Alexander Solzenitzen survived cancer in the Gulag with the help of kombucha. Synthetic interferons formulated into drugs are prescribed not only for cancer, but also for my health problems, which are labelled as multiple sclerosis. In the case of MS, they are self-injected several times a week at a cost of up to $23,000 a year. They are not a cure but put some people into a holding pattern for a few years. They make some people sicker, but such negative case history data are not systematically collected or disseminated.

Within months of being told I had MS, fatigue forced me to stop working. When I told my father this news, he asked me what I was doing to help myself. I told him I was approaching my health with a variety of holistic treatments.

"I'm glad to hear it," he said, "because if you let those doctors get ahold of you, you'll just get worse."

My father was then over ninety years old, a tough old farmer who still lived alone, cooked for himself and held a valid, if restricted, driver's license. He had been well-coached by my mother, who had been the traditional healer for our area. So I came by my perspectives honestly.

My health problems advanced quickly, and I was soon in a wheelchair. Again, I responded to bad news with activism. I researched how to support my health holistically, shared my findings in articles published by the MS Society and started a book of MS health recovery stories. Conventional medical doctors tell us that there is no known cause or cure for MS. However, I had no trouble finding people who had restored their health with holistic approaches involving detoxification, diet and lifestyle change among other things. Each recovery story is a unique journey back to health, and none of them would fit the double blind, placebo-controlled study model developed to test drugs. Most medical practitioners now believe this is the only way to find trustworthy information, but even without such studies, the stories of MS recovery are very real.

The story about the kombucha recovery received a torrent of responses. My telephone and email brought new inquiries for weeks. I couldn't help smiling as I gave out kombucha babies and the recipe for making "folk" interferons at home from black tea and white sugar for pennies a day. I thought as I smiled, *Too bad, Rockefeller. Another $23,000 a year you'll miss out on.*

My story caught the attention of conventional medical personnel as well. A letter to the MS Society from someone with a doctoral degree in pharmacology said MS had been "targeted" by kombucha "advocates." The writer stated that the tea had killed at least one person and had many negative side effects, and he backed these claims with citations from well-known medical journals. I checked every citation before writing a politely devastating response. I pointed out that the facts in the articles cited did not support the claim of death caused by kombucha, which is easily found on the internet. A person who drank kombucha did die, but the autopsy found a bowel puncture. Such punctures are usually fatal.

I treasure another result of my incursion into territory conventional medicine claims as its own. My article was discussed at a national board meeting of the MS Society. It seems the main concern was whether the society would bear any legal liability from any actions that might arise from my story. The final result was a decision to place a disclaimer on every page of every future article or web page published by the MS Society. I smile whenever I think of someone suing because they recovered their health.

The Rockefeller interests won't miss any profits kombucha might take away, I'm sure. But these new memories make my own long journey back to health and walking feel easier. The old activist in me is only too happy to be able to say, "Chalk up one for the little guys."

PEEING WITH DISTINCTION

In that old Potter's Shop I stood alone
With the clay Population round in Rows.
And, strange to tell, among that Earthen Lot
Some could articulate, while others not:
And suddenly one more impatient cried —
"Who is the Potter, pray, and who the Pot?"
…after Silence spake
A Vessel of a more ungainly Make:
"They sneer at me for leaning all awry;
What! did the Hand, then, of the Potter shake?"

Ruba'iyat by Omar Khayyam

Telemarketers calling to solicit donations almost never get money from my number, but they keep calling anyway. It doesn't matter how often I tell them that my health challenges make me the main charity at my house or how often I ask to be removed from their lists. I sometimes wonder if they keep calling because they've heard that I once raised $500 for the Young Women's Christian Association YW even though I'm neither young nor Christian.

It all started innocently enough. Every year the YW holds a gala dinner where they give out awards called "Woman of Distinction." It's a bit like the Academy Awards in that there are categories such as Health and Wellness, Entrepreneurship, Science and Technology, and Medicine (as distinct from Health and Wellness, but my biases are showing).

One year I was nominated for a Woman of Distinction award in the Health and Wellness category. The friends who nominated me thought my work integrating holistic or "alternative" health perspectives into the Multiple Sclerosis Society was worthy of recognition. I felt honoured and agreed before I fully understood that nomination made me a pawn in the fundraising game. A condition of nomination is attendance at the awards banquet, and I was encouraged to invite friends and family at $100 a head to attend with me. Five paying guests decided to accompany me: my nominator; my husband, Michael; my editor from the MS Society; and two friends who have also been diagnosed with MS.

Living life in a wheelchair as I did at the time, I was used to checking and double-checking the accessibility of any potential destination, especially the toilets. My bladder ruled my life. When it gave me its signal, I only had a few minutes to get in position to do its bidding. I knew that the hotel hosting the dinner had a wheelchair-accessible washroom on the ground floor, and I asked about the one on the floor where the dinner would be held.

"No problem," I was told.

I assumed "no problem" meant there was an accessible toilet on the same floor. Although I knew that assuming was risky, I never got around to casing the premises before the actual event. After all, the hotel was a Hyatt. I also understood the YW had assigned someone to liaise with the hotel in advance about my special needs, so I assumed all eventualities were covered.

On the night of the dinner, Michael and I arrived at the appointed time. I was given a nominees' badge with a yellow daffodil on it to distinguish me. It was May, after all. Because of my disability, it was agreed that Michael would accompany me to the "nominees only" reception.

We were told the public elevators were switched off to help control access to the awards event but that a hotel staff person would get us up to the reception by another route. A pleasant young man arrived to guide us. It turned out the alternative route was via a freight elevator and a kitchen. We followed our guide to the back of the foyer, round a dividing wall and into a very large elevator. He inserted at key behind a small door in the elevator wall and pressed a button.

As we began a slow ascent, I asked our guide if there was a wheelchair-accessible washroom on the floor to which he was taking us. He answered "no," but added that if I wanted to make a stop now, there was a washroom on our route. I didn't know how the evening would unfold, so it seemed prudent to make the stop while I had the opportunity.

Our guide escorted us to an area of the hotel I recognized as the mezzanine level where I used to meet friends for Sunday brunch. The disabled toilet was part of the "normal" women's washroom. Opening the door, my wheelchair-sensitive eyes saw a very narrow hallway immediately behind it. Before leaving Michael, I told him the lack of space beside the door meant I would not be able to open it to exit the washroom without help. We agreed he would wait outside, and I would tap a code on the door when I needed it opened—a sort of disabled "open sesame."

My cubicle had its own private sink and appeared to be a recent conversion of two regular cubicles into one large one, and the grab bar was appropriately placed for me to get out of and back into my wheelchair easily. So far, so good. I tapped the magic code, and the door opened for me as planned. We rejoined our guide and continued our journey to the nominees' reception.

After another slow ascent, the elevator opened into the biggest kitchen I've ever seen. It was empty but for us and rows and rows of gleaming stainless steel counters, stovetops and sinks. Huge pots and pans hung in wait above them. Large black and white tiles covered the floor; a mop in a great bucket stood in a corner, evidence of its recent cleaning. It felt like a world in waiting, even a little surreal without any sounds or smells of cooking, or culinary masters in high white hats. We passed through a door at the kitchen's farthest end and, abruptly it seemed, found ourselves in the reception room.

Here, some fifty people stood close to tables that ringed the room. The tables were covered with nearly empty trays of vegetables, cheese, crackers and definitely empty steam trays that had probably held hot hors d'oeuvre. Two young women wearing hotel badges presided over a table with bottles of wine and glasses. They smiled, offering us drinks. Subdued laughter and conversation filled the background as someone at a microphone thanked the corporate sponsors of the event.

Over the next few minutes, each of the nominees was introduced and walked forward or waved in acknowledgement. The reception ended shortly after the introductions, and we were taken via the kitchen to another elevator that took us up to the event floor.

We encountered the reception for paying guests and found that our table mates, who didn't all know one another, had nonetheless come together. We waited to enter our dining room until the crowd at the doorway died down. Inside we found a massive, echoing conference room full of round tables covered with white cloths and decorated with baskets of spring flowers—irises, daffodils and hyacinths. We sat near the door, at the back of the room.

My companions enjoyed an appetizer followed by either a chicken or prawn dinner and dessert. I had requested salmon with vegetables in advance. Had it been a normal night at home, I would have finished eating three hours before we started at this event. I knew my body would make no allowance for the special occasion and would wake me up at 4:00 a.m. in pain and spasm if I ate too much, too late, or the wrong foods. So I ate very lightly and declined dessert.

The editor of the MS Society journals for which I wrote made a very touching speech. He said whether I was selected by the judges of this event as "the" Health and Wellness Woman of Distinction, I was special, a winner in his eyes and those of everyone else at the table. He took a series of photographs to help us all remember the occasion.

Then the pre-award speeches began at the microphone. My husband suggested this would be the right time to visit the washroom again as we had been at the table almost ninety minutes and might be there for some time yet. We were directed to the women's washroom on our floor. Inside, however, I found there was no disabled cubicle. Back outside with Michael, we asked if the public elevators were now functional. The answer was still "no," so it was back to the freight elevators. It seemed no one had thought these elevators would be required again, and the necessary keys were no longer available. Someone was dispatched to find them and returned just as I was beginning to think Michael might have to come into the regular washroom with me and stand in as my grab bar.

Instead, we made another trip through the now familiar black-and-white floored kitchen. The mezzanine level was empty so Michael pushed me over the long stretch of carpet inside the washroom as I was now a bit desperate. There was no one else around, but the keeper of the keys remained outside and had promised to warn any comers about Michael's presence in the women's washroom. As we made our way once again to the freight elevator to rejoin the awards dinner, I was starting to feel rather distinct, but not particularly honoured.

Back at our table, we found we had missed the award and acceptance speeches for all the categories before mine. As the nominee names for the Health and Wellness award were read out, I felt a small tingle of anticipation through my building fatigue. I felt winning was a long shot because my work focused on alternative approaches to health and wellness; I guessed I was more than a little ahead of my time. When I heard the panel of judges announced, I was sure they would have chosen someone more conventional than me. And they had. A sixty-something academic who had written a book about women who encountered harassment from the male medical establishment. The award process wound slowly to a close as we all screened yawns behind our hands and said our goodbyes.

Michael and I decided to try the ground floor washroom on our way out as we guessed that retrieving our car from the valet parking might be a lengthy process. The public elevators were finally operating again, so we made our way to the ground floor without having to pass through the echoing kitchen. We arrived at the washroom door to find a sign telling us that it was closed for repairs. We decided to go in anyhow and check out how restrictive the repairs were to the accessible toilet.

We found the cubicle without a door or tiles on the floor, but the toilet appeared to be functional. I decided to use it as is. Michael kept watch from near the door. With my bladder happy again, we made our way to the valet parking desk and handed in our ticket. We were told we'd have about a half-hour wait for our car. Michael and I shared a knowing look, having had our decision about braving the washroom construction validated. I chatted with other nominees who were waiting as well, and the time seemed to pass quickly enough.

I was more than ready to leave when our car finally arrived. In half an hour we were home and brushing our teeth in preparation for a very welcome bed.

The telephone rang at midnight and Michael asked if I was expecting a call, and if I thought he should answer.

Thinking of my ninety-something father and Michael's aging parents in England, he answered the phone. The caller turned out to be a man from Australia who had made a twelve-hour error in calculating the time difference to Canada. He explained that his doctors had advised him to get his affairs in order as they did not expect him to survive beyond one year given the severity of the complicating factors in his case. An internet search turned up an article I'd written for the MS Society about a man with MS who had recovered his health by having a special form of ostrich oil rubbed on his body every day. More remarkable was the fact that he began with severe pain and had spent years in a wheelchair but was pain-free and walking—indeed, happily mowing his lawn—after three months of the treatment. The caller had tracked me down through the telephone directory assistance service. His wife had MS, and they were looking for further details on the person who had recovered and the source of the oil.

The caller was very apologetic when he realized how late it was for us. He said he'd arrange for his wife to call me the next day. However, before he hung up he thanked me for my story, saying it had given him and his wife hope that was otherwise missing in their lives. Their doctors had told them MS was "incurable."

Michael and I were relieved that neither of our families were calling with bad news. Through my exhaustion, I couldn't help feeling flattered by the call from Australia. The YWCA's selection panel had not chosen me as their

Woman of Distinction, however, someone I'd never meet from the other side of the world had found what I did to be worthwhile, inspiring and a rare source of that precious commodity—hope.

I fell asleep smiling about my bathroom adventures through the hotel's kitchen and a construction site. While it didn't fit any Woman of Distinction award category, the hotel made sure I peed with distinction.

ADVENTURES WITH JACKIE

My friend Jackie heard I was working on a book of stories about things that can only happen to people with a chronic illness or incapacity of some sort. Jackie has never allowed creeping disability to get in the way of fully living life. She laughs where others might let fear or embarrassment seep in and dampen the chance to feel joy. She takes pride in the crazy situations in which she regularly finds herself and is open to everything life offers. Jackie especially loves to travel to places even those with able bodies think twice about.

To get her full share of the fifteen minutes of fame Andy Warhol promised us all, Jackie asked me to tell my readers about her adventures in order that they may see that disability isn't a death sentence.

The following six stories are meant to do just that.

DOUBLE DOORS

Experience is the name everyone gives to their mistakes.

Lady Windermere's Fan by Oscar Wilde

J ackie had always approached life as an adventure, but with her advancing disabilities, comical situations occurred regularly. Fortunately, the pickles she got herself into caused her little embarrassment.

She called me one day to tell me about her latest escapade but began by saying she needed an excuse to avoid the housework and to ignore her bed and the ever-present job of tidying it.

"The public rooms of my apartment—the sitting room and the bathroom—I keep neat and normal, but my bedroom is another story," she said. "The computer is in one corner, and the bed doubles as a desk. Clothes from the last two days are on the bed waiting to be worn again to different places with different people, or for the laundry. I just haven't decided which yet and can't get to the closet to hang them up because the clothes from last week are still in front of the door waiting to be washed."

She told me this was why she likes going to a natural hot spring in the bush where she doesn't have to wear clothes if she doesn't want to. That adventure creates no laundry.

Her bills are on the edge of the bed waiting to be paid. She's pretty good at that as long as she has her calendar to remind her of the date. But the weeks just seem to fly by. Christmases seemed so far apart when she was a kid, and now it seems one lot of Christmas shopping just ends before the carols are on the radio again.

Jackie's desk (a.k.a. the bed) holds a pen, a scissors, a box of tissues, two cups, a digital camera, a spoon and an empty yoghurt pot, a deck of cards, several (unlabelled) floppy discs and an empty pill container.

"There *is* room on the far side of the bed to sleep, but it's a good thing I'm not a restless sleeper," she laughed.

Jackie continued her saga by explaining that she keeps her scooter by her apartment door so it is handy for shopping at the local store. If she needs to go farther, she loads her scooter into her camper van which has a lift that picks up the scooter and deposits it behind the front seats. That morning, Jackie had left her apartment in her scooter and was headed to the parking garage, but she ran into a little glitch on her way out to get into her van to go meet a friend.

I'll let Jackie take over from here:

The hallway from the elevator to the parking garage has two fire doors to get through to my van. The fire doors are spaced only four feet apart, so I have to pull the first door toward me to open it on the way out of the building. The building manager had always left the inside door open for me. It opened into the hall approach, and the outside one opened into the four-foot space between them. But when the fire marshal tightened the door closers, the apartment manager was warned he had to keep both doors closed.

On my way to the garage on my scooter today, I had to open the inside door and move forward to grab the handle of the outer door to pull it toward me while trying to keep the inside door open with my scooter so I could back up while pulling the outer door toward me. I don't know how it happened, but the inner door closed, shutting me in the space between the two doors. My three-foot-long scooter was now trapped in the four-foot space between the doors. The door into the parking garage was now impossible to open from inside with the scooter filling the space. So I waited and hoped someone else would soon be going to the garage and could let me out. Thirty minutes later, I was still in the four-foot space, and my impatience was growing. That triggered my brain to remember that I had my cell phone in my pocket, so I dialled 911.

The operator asked what service I wanted, and when she heard I was stuck between two doors, she laughed and said she'd send the fire department. I imagined hearing a distant siren as I waited for my rescuers, even though I knew they wouldn't use a siren for the kind of rescue. Not long afterward the inside door opened, and a kind voice said, "You can back out now, ma'am."

I backed out and saw a tall man wearing yellow gum boots, a face mask and a big yellow hat holding a bar in his hand. If I hadn't known he was there to rescue me, I would have thought he looked a little scary. After a few deep breaths I told the fireman I felt like a canned sardine in that little hallway, and a bit claustrophobic. The fireman asked if I was all right, and after assuring him that I was fine now that I was free (except for feeling a bit silly), he held the inside door so I could open the outside door into the parking garage and make my exit.

Once in the parking garage I drove out to my camper, loaded the scooter and got on with the day. *Thank heaven for the firemen*, I thought to myself. *Not all their work is dangerous, but if I'd had to stay in that hallway a lot longer, I'd have kissed him when he opened the door for me.*

THE KINDNESS OF STRANGERS

> Experience teaches me by facts what study teaches me by theory. The only way for me to convert theory into fact is through experience. Experience is the purest form of knowledge.
>
> Anonymous

Jackie's had an adventurous streak most of her adult life. Chronic illness has been with her almost as long, but she's never let it stop her from going somewhere she really wanted to go or doing something she really wanted to do. She's learned that if she can't get herself out of a jam, it's just a matter of time before someone comes along and offers help.

Jackie met her friend Marian on a trip to Europe and later went to visit Marian's family in Nigeria. In fact, she almost became Marian's father's third wife. But that's another story. Marian became Jackie's travel partner at home too. Jackie bought a camper van to make exercising her adventurous streak easier, especially when wilderness is involved.

After a winter of dark, rainy days, Jackie's travel itch just had to be scratched, so she and Marian decided to go as far west as they could on the first spring long weekend. Although Jackie's children are now having travel adventures of their own, she always remembers one of their nannies who was from a tiny place at the edge of the Western world. On the western end of the Trans-Canada Highway is a town called Port Renfrew, if you can find it on the map. When fishing and logging were still viable industries in this part of the world, there may have been five hundred people living there. Now that tourism has replaced the old resource industries, Port Renfrew is known as the southern end of the West Coast Trail. Cut through the coastal rainforest, the trail offers unparalleled views as well as physical challenges. A little further back in history, it was built as a life-saving trail for the poor souls shipwrecked off the rugged western shores of Vancouver Island.

The kind of challenge this trail presents has always struck Jackie as a bit masochistic, but she wanted to see the beach just south of Port Renfrew—Botanical Beach, the nanny called it. You have to time a visit with the low tide, she said. Otherwise it's just another view of the waves rolling in across the Pacific from Asia. If you're lucky you might see spouts from resident grey whales. But at low tide, Botanical Beach is transformed. Its smooth sandstone floor is pitted with depressions, some as big as hot tubs (but not as pleasant to sit in). There are depressions within depressions, all of them teeming with life of one shape or another, and sometimes very prickly life, like sea urchins. Other life forms are so tiny you need a magnifying glass to see them. And there's every size and shape in between. Perhaps this is why it is also designated a nature reserve and is under study by a number of universities.

With this kind of mystique, Botanical Beach was the real destination on this particular sunny spring weekend. The urban sites of Victoria would make a pleasant prelude.

As Port Renfrew is on Vancouver Island, Jackie and Marian had to hop a ferry to get there. This is one of the few times it is an advantage to have a disability. When the ferry terminal staff see a "disabled" sign, the vehicle is waved to the front of the line. They also make sure to park it next to the elevator, with enough space behind for the scooter lift. Jackie can walk, but not very far or very fast.

The ferry skirted between Galiano Island and Maine Island, then nipped into the harbour at Schwartz Bay, a spectacularly beautiful ninety-minute cruise. Marian and Jackie had breakfast and then went out on deck to see if they could spot some bald eagles or passing killer whales. They were lucky on both counts that day.

Victoria is the capital city of the province of British Columbia. The legislative buildings were built in the late nineteenth century and have the pomp and solidity of empire about them. Other remnants of the colonial era give Victoria the quaint feel that makes it a tourist mecca. Its location at the edge of the sea gives it great views and clean air. Marian and Jackie visited Butchart Gardens, a green thumb's delight. At one time a stone quarry, it's now a lush mixture of rainforest and romantic garden. The rhododendrons were in full, glorious bloom.

But Port Renfrew was calling, so they headed west along a narrow highway following the water's edge. It was getting dark, so they turned off at a sign for a campground at Sooke Potholes Regional Park. Marian found its location in the forest up the side of a mountain a bit too wild and didn't want to stay there. It was too far into the bush for her, and the sign warning of a cougar in the area didn't help. She probably thought there'd be pot smokers there, too, given the name. They weren't planning to get out of the camper, but Marian just couldn't get comfortable with the idea of spending the night in the forest.

Marian had seen a Catholic church back on the highway dedicated to Our Lady of Lima, one of her favourite saints, and she really wanted to go to mass the next morning. So they headed back to the church and pulled into the parking lot. They asked a man walking by if he thought anyone would mind if they slept there. Marian assured him she was Catholic and suggested he could call her priest if he needed to verify this. The man said he didn't think Our Lady of Lima would mind, and anyhow the church was on First Nations' land. He was a council member, so could say it was okay. They took his name just in case they had to tell someone they had permission to park there. So between God and the First Nations, Jackie and Marian had a place for the night where they both felt comfortable.

They woke up at 10:00 a.m. for the 10:30 mass. The parishioners stared at the camper van as they filed in. Marian and Jackie threw their clothes on and joined them. As Marian went to communion, she looked down and let out a gasp. She was wearing one of Jackie's running shoes and one of her own. Jackie's were equally mismatched. She laughed and wondered what the sedately attired parishioners thought. With their camping clothes and mismatched shoes, they looked more like hobos—or maybe winos.

However, the friendly parishioners offered tea and cakes after the service, and Jackie and Marian had a chance to show they were nice women despite their disheveled appearance. The parishioners were amazed by Marian's weave hairdo. Not only is she Nigerian, but her greying black hair has shoulder-length dark reddish and blue braids woven into it. Despite her difference in this remote Caucasian place, Marian's beauty and integrity made her the centre of attention, and although there were a few furtive glances at their shoes, no one said anything. They were good Christian people.

Back on the highway, the ladies drove an hour on a twisted road that reminded Jackie of the road to Hana on Maui. She had to keep a tight hold on both the steering wheel and her stomach contents. Because of the pitch of the road, she had to shift into first or second gear (in an automatic!) to get up and down some of the hills.

They drove through a town called Sooke, and then Jordan River, and then an hour more. Jackie had no idea it would be so far from Victoria. Still in the forest, they came to a small collection of houses strung along the road where a sign indicated they were in Port Renfrew and at the end of the Trans-Canada Highway.

Following the signs to Botanical Beach, Jackie felt she had also reached the end of the world. The road kept getting narrower and narrower, steeper and steeper, and the tarmac turned to gravel. A small parking lot was as far as she could go in her low-slung camper van.

Jackie was determined to go the rest of the way to the beach on her scooter, so they asked a local in the parking lot which would be the easiest route to take. Feeling relatively confident that Jackie could make it, they headed down the trail. It was part amusement park ride and part obstacle course as Jackie whizzed down the trail on her scooter. Steps and roots and wooden bridges three feet wide are no problem to a walker, but on a scooter that's two feet, ten inches wide, it's a tightwire act to manoeuvre over. But Jackie proved it possible.

Near the bottom of the hill, there was a wooden bridge with two steps at the end just wider than Jackie's scooter. She should have stopped there but really wanted to see the beach that had drawn her so far from civilization. And see it she would! Marian kept asking if Jackie's scooter had enough power and always heard, "Sure. No problem." Jackie completely forgot that it hadn't been recharged for two days. She had driven it around Victoria for four hours, up and down hills. And, of course, the church parking lot had no electricity to plug it into overnight as she usually did.

The vegetation along the trail had turned to lush salal, and the trees had that bonsai look from the constant upward winds from the Pacific. Jackie knew the beach wasn't far now. She could hear the surf pounding. There was an opening a little farther along. When she stood up she could see over the top of the bush to the open ocean. Jackie felt like she was looking out to China.

She spent another ten minutes fighting her way over roots and stumps down the trail. She could see the beach and the beautiful, flat, weather-beaten black rock and the tidal pools, but it was still another one hundred feet down. The trail was impossible for her scooter, even with her determination, so she contented herself with the aroma of salt air and the sound of pounding surf. She sat there for half an hour. The trip was worth every inch as far as she was concerned. The incoming tide crept closer to the pools that she would have loved to see up close and explore.

Marian was worried about the trip back up the hill. When Jackie turned the scooter around and started up the trail, the scooter had had enough and barely inched along to make its point.

Marian had an "I told you so" look on her face, but she didn't say anything. She tried valiantly to push Jackie along the rough trail, and Jackie walked as much as she could.

"It won't be long," she said encouragingly. "Just watch, someone will come along and help push me."

She had gained some weight and was close to two hundred pounds, but Marian was strong, determined and wearing her now-matched running shoes. She rested every three minutes or so, which meant it would be nightfall before they made it back to the parking lot.

In the first half hour, only two groups passed Jackie and Marian. They helped them over two six-inch-high roots and the steps at the end of the bridge. But then they carried on up the trail ahead of them. Eventually, Jackie's scooter just flatly refused to move at all. The ladies sat for ten minutes hoping the scooter would recharge a little. They started up again, stopping every minute for a ten-minute rest. Marian is a math whiz, and she calculated that it would take about four hours to get to the parking lot with just the two of them at the rate they were going. She wasn't an outdoorsy kind of person, and Jackie saw her jump a couple of times when a branch fell to the ground. She crossed herself more than once. No doubt she was calling on Our Lady of Lima for help.

Her prayers were answered when Gary and Elaine came marching up the hill behind them. They asked if the ladies wanted help, and Marian said, "Yes, bless you." She crossed herself one more time.

Gary had the build of a football player, and Jackie's bulk didn't seem to concern him. He turned out to be a physical education student and obviously was very physically fit. He looked like an angel to the ladies. He reassured them that they would be back up the hill in no time. And he was right. On the way, they found out that Gary and Elaine were students at the University of Victoria out to enjoy the beauty of the beach. It took only about thirty minutes of pushing and resting before they saw the welcome sight of the van in the parking lot.

"So long," Gary and Elaine said as if the help they gave was just a natural part of the day's adventures for them.

It had been a fun, fast ride down the hill until they hit the bush and the roots. Although Jackie hadn't gazed into the tidal pools herself, Elaine described the highlights for her on the push back up the hill. Jackie was sure she'd never forget the beautiful sight of the beach and the waves or the salt air and the sound of the waves crashing in the distance.

She's sure her memories would be different if it hadn't been for the kindness of strangers, yet again. She said a prayer of thanks to Our Lady of Lima, and then pointed the camper east, starting the drive back toward the city. It's called "civilization," but it felt like it might be a touch boring after the adventures in the wild. Gary and Elaine had brought their own version of civilization to the daunting bush adventure in the help they gave without thought of any return. Marian sat exhausted and quiet in the seat beside Jackie. Jackie smiled and thought, *I'm the queen of the end of the road.*

INTO AFRICA

Leg problems often indicate a fear of moving forward or a reluctance to move forward in a certain direction.

Louise Hay

Jackie's girlfriend, Marian, is Nigerian. Marian's father, John, came to Canada on an extended visit of six months. Marian had just been promoted and was working long hours to make a good impression on her new boss, which meant John wasn't seeing much beyond Marian's neighbourhood, so Jackie decided to play tour guide. They started by going for drives, but as Jackie got to know him, she decided to make it her job to ensure that he experienced all the things that make living on the west coast of Canada different to Nigeria.

John was seventy-five and Jackie was fifty at the time. She travelled with a scooter that she could load in her van. It worked out that the two of them moved at virtually the same speed, so Jackie felt all was going well. She found out just how well after four months of touring with John. He told Jackie with a very serious look on his face that he felt Jackie would make a good third wife and he would be honoured if she would marry him. As a Nigerian, he is legally permitted to have more than one wife, so he asked if Jackie would go back to Nigeria with him when his time in Canada was over. Flattered and very amused, Jackie gently told him she couldn't marry him, but that she would try to visit him in Africa.

A year later, Marian told Jackie she was going home to Nigeria to visit her family and asked if Jackie would like to come along. Jackie thought it was a great opportunity and enthusiastically said yes. She felt this might be her only chance to travel to Africa and feel safe as she'd be with people she could trust. They'd stay with Marian's family, who would guide Jackie through problems with money exchange and all the other details of being a disabled tourist using a mobility scooter.

Jackie decided to ask her two daughters, Christine (twenty) and Laura (twenty-one) if they wanted to come along, and they jumped at the chance. Both of them were beautiful women with long blonde hair and blue eyes. After the deal was already done, Jackie wondered if she was crazy to even think of taking them to a country filled with sexy young black men. But Christine and Laura were dedicated students on summer break from their university programs, so Jackie felt confident they would come back to continue their studies. Her daughters assured her they'd be able to earn enough money during the coming year to cover their tuition, and they all felt travelling to another continent would be a learning experience.

Jackie also wanted to take her daughters with her because of her brain fog, a very sneaky thing. She may look alert at times, but her brain had gone into what she calls "tilt"—it just doesn't compute—and she could end up anywhere. She might get into the wrong part of the airport and miss her plane or end up on a flight to Timbuktu. But with Marian, Christine and Laura all there to look out for her, Jackie felt she should survive even a thirty-six-hour journey.

When they finally arrived at the airport in the Nigerian capital, Lagos, Marian said they should stay together and wait until her brothers arrived before leaving the terminal building. The four suitcases they had checked in Canada arrived on the luggage carousel promptly, but the five pieces that were Jackie's scooter—her legs—were nowhere to be seen. Marian guided them to the information desk and explained what they were missing. A staff member took them behind the high wall of their counter, and there was Jackie's scooter, safe and already assembled. She was happy to have some independence again as the wheelchair on which she came off the airplane needed someone to push her. It had no hand rims to allow Jackie to manoeuvre herself.

Two of Marian's brothers, accompanied by their body guards, were waiting outside the glass doors of the arrival hall. Marian said the glass was bulletproof, which didn't make Jackie feel any safer, and her brothers obviously weren't taking any chances either. More fatigued from the journey than she remembered ever feeling, Jackie stayed close to Marian and her brothers on her scooter.

Looking down the walkway from the arrival terminal to the parking lot, Jackie saw hundreds of disabled men, hands outstretched, begging. Some were missing one foot and moved with crutches. Some had only one arm or one hand. There were even some men missing both legs who lay on a sort of skateboard and pushed themselves around with their hands. Jackie felt guilty that she had a luxurious vehicle that allowed her to sit in comfort and use only a thumb to press the accelerator and carry her wherever she wanted to go. Jackie was very glad to be with Marian's brothers and their guards, as she felt more than a little intimidated by the scene. Marian, Christine, Laura and Jackie had taken off their jewelry so they weren't presenting tempting targets; their money was tied around their waists and stuffed in their bras.

A beggar reached an arm toward Jackie through the guards with a few coins in his hand. Without thinking, she took the coins and said, "Thank you." The beggar gasped and pulled his hand back, looking at it with a stunned expression. He turned and ran. The others saw what had happened, and suddenly the whole avenue of beggars began melting away from the path. By the time they reached the parking lot, there were none to be seen.

It was Christine and Laura who figured things out first. They asked Marian if the reason so many young men were missing hands, arms, feet or legs was because of a traditional Islamic punishment. Nigeria has a substantial Muslim population in the north. Her answer was a quiet "yes." It dawned on Jackie that she was now a thief too. She hoped the beggar hadn't gone for a policeman.

Marian's brothers dismantled Jackie's scooter and loaded it and the luggage in one car. The four of them and one of Marian's brothers climbed into another car and left the airport parking lot. Jackie didn't see any police officers along the way, so her foggy head guessed the beggar hadn't informed on her. Nonetheless, she made a mental note to be careful when they left Nigeria in case any of the beggars recognized her.

A few weeks later, they left Lagos Airport via the same terminal. Jackie had a much clearer head. The beggars were still there, and she returned the coins she'd collected on arrival several times over. While they were still of great interest to the beggars, they encountered no problems. *Thank heaven,* Jackie thought. *I'd hate to lose a hand over the equivalent of fourteen cents.*

VILLAGE LIFE IN NIGERIA

Truth is never pure, and rarely simple.

From *The Importance of Being Earnest*
by Oscar Wilde

Marian's brothers, James and Paul, took to Jackie's daughters as Jackie was afraid they would. At the end of the first week, Christine was presented with an engagement ring, and Laura began working out plans for a business importing cars into Nigeria from Europe. The time seemed right to leave the city and visit Marian's father, John, in his village. Jackie hoped her daughters would forget James' and Paul's efforts to have them stay in Lagos.

The night before they left Lagos, James, who had presented Christine with an engagement ring, came up with a scheme he hoped would get her to stay with him. He made a bet with Christine that he could beat her at pool. If he won she would marry him; if he lost he would go to a karaoke bar with Christine and sing a song of her choosing.

Laura and Jackie shared a knowing look. Christine was a pool shark, and they knew they didn't have to worry about leaving her behind. Still, they waited anxiously to hear the outcome of the bet. Around midnight, the gate of the compound opened and James and Christine joined them in the sitting room. Seeing the questioning looks, James said, a little sheepishly, a little sadly, "I sang 'Yellow Bird' at the karaoke bar."

They left Lagos to drive to Oboluoko in the interior of Nigeria. Marian's family was the biggest in the village and had the largest house, so they exerted the most influence. Her father was called Sir John, and since he did not own a car, drivers with cars for hire parked close to his compound in case he might want to go to Lagos or Benin, cities where he had children.

As visitors from Canada, Jackie, Laura and Christine were the object of much attention in Oboluoko. Jackie rode her Moby scooter, and people in the markets were amazed to see a large white woman rolling around on this low version of a luxury tricycle. A crowd usually formed to follow Jackie while she shopped. Women liked to put their babies on Jackie's lap and then indicate she should have her companions take a picture. The photographer would then be asked to pay for the picture of the baby. The babies were all adorable, but Jackie soon started to ask herself, *How many baby pictures do I need?* When she stopped having pictures taken, the crowd following her got smaller.

John's compound had twenty-two rooms, one for each of his twenty-two "children." Marian's mother and Momma Aimee, his second wife, both lived in the compound. They seemed unconcerned that John had asked Jackie to become his third wife. She was ready to explain that she had no intention of becoming a third wife, but no one ever raised the subject. Marian explained that Aimee was John's deceased brother's wife, and that ten of the children her father provided for were actually her cousins. Others were "half-siblings," a term that seemed to be used a bit loosely to include many extended family members in need of a home. Jackie could only conclude that John saw a marriage with her as a way of helping him provide for his family. Families operate as a social security net in Nigeria where the state takes no role in providing the social services a North American or European takes for granted.

Life was rustic in the village, as water was heated on a wood fire and then carried to her by a woman who balanced the jar on top of her head. She'd fill a basin this way twice a day so Jackie could wash. There was one flushing toilet close to John's room, and all the rest were pit toilets. The family's animals lived in the compound too. Little goats ran freely, and a flock of chickens pecked up anything that looked like food. Nobody paid them much attention. Most of the compound's rooms were empty as the majority of the children had grown up and moved to the cities. The goats took over one bedroom at night and the chickens another. After the first night, Jackie was moved to a bedroom at the far end of the compound as she snores and was disturbing both the people and the animals.

One weekend there was to be a soccer game between the church women of Oboluoko and another village just up the Niger River. On Sunday morning, the women came to Sir John to tell him they would have to forfeit the game because one of their players was sick. Laura heard of the problem, and as she had played high school soccer, offered to help out. The team members sang their joy when they heard Laura would play for them and they wouldn't have to forfeit their game after all.

Although no beating drums announced the start of the game, people from neighbouring villages started to show up to watch the soccer game. The word must have spread that a pretty blue-eyed goddess staying in Sir John's compound was playing. Although it felt like they were about as far away from a technological civilization as they could get, someone brought a video camera and filmed the game, which turned out to be very exciting. Laura played well and scored a goal. She did a header, took the knocks and slashes and gave as good as she got. The crowd was impressed. Laura said later she wouldn't have guessed that fifty-year-old church women would play as determinedly, even viciously, as these women did.

Laura survived the game without injury and is now something of a legend in Oboluoko. We've heard that the movie of the game is shown once a year in the summer. Crowds gather in the little village church to watch the video of the white girl helping the women's team of Oboluoku win their game.

MY AFRICAN STEROTYPE: WILD MONKEYS

> I am the only person in the world I should like to
> know thoroughly.
>
> *Lady Windermere's Fan* by Oscar Wilde

When the day came to take leave of Marian's parents' home near the village of Oboluoko, they hired a Volkswagen that was parked near Sir John's compound. They had four large suitcases and Jackie's scooter to consider, and they ended up tying two of the suitcases on top. The car looked pregnant with four of them and their bags squeezed in along with the driver. Their destination was Marian's sister's compound in the city of Benin, a three-hour drive away. They arrived at an elegant compound with a high wall around it and a gatekeeper.

Marian's sister had ten to fifteen servants, apparently all cousins, who did the housekeeping and cooking among other things. Jackie was sure she came as close as she ever would to being treated like a queen. A houseboy always seemed to know what she wanted and came running if she needed to put on her shoes or take them off. Jackie commented she hadn't seen a single monkey—nor, in fact, had she seen any jungle or wild animals in Nigeria, stereotypes she associated with Africa. Marian's sister decided to take her to the local zoo, which was the only place she knew she'd find a monkey.

The Benin Zoo held a small variety of animals in chicken wire cages. Jackie was interested to see a cage said to be holding an American bald eagle, but she was sure it was a vulture. When she got to the monkey enclosure, there were two monkeys on the opposite side. Jackie approached the cage making a little noise with her mouth. Maybe it was her cane, her scooter or her chirping noise, but one monkey ran to meet her, swung its arm over the fence and punched her in the face from two feet away. The monkey's arm must have been three feet long! Jackie crumpled to the ground.

People came running and helped her up. They were all very shocked. Jackie's eyes were full of dirt and, she feared, monkey droppings. She suddenly realized monkeys were not the cleanest animals, and certainly not very cuddly. Luckily it was only her ego that was injured, and her stereotypes. Maybe it was all the *National Geographic* specials she'd seen on TV, but she had an image of herself in Africa playing with a cuddly monkey.

Back on her feet, Jackie and the monkeys had a brief stare-down. Perhaps she looked like a zoo creature to them with her white skin. She decided then and there that she preferred the picture of monkeys she saw on television, and that in the future she would always stay more than three feet away from a cage of monkeys.

A SCOOTER IS NOT A JEEP

Today, I invite you to begin a new season
where we can dream
that everything we undertake is possible
and we fulfill it,
with joy and dignity.

Anonymous

Jackie's daughter Christine had just purchased a jeep, so they decided to attend a jeep jamboree at Apex Mountain where Christine could learn her limits and how to drive the back roads safely. Being a responsible mom, Jackie wanted to encourage the correct attitude. Even though Jackie had driven a jeep for years, she never knew there were as many types as she encountered at the jamboree. Some had regular tires, some had capital L, Large, tires. You know the ones. They make the vehicle look like a giant crab or spider. The vehicle looks like it could drive over you without ruffling a hair in your "do."

The first day of the jamboree, Christine took the jeep 101 course. They had to climb an almost vertical hill, go over the top, and then down the other side in low gear. The next test was to sit on the side of a hill at a thirty-degree angle, and Jackie was on the lower side of the jeep. She just held on, prayed and looked down at the valley below.

There were several other skills Christine had to learn before she could leave for the mountain tops, mud holes and creeks. It was a wonderful day, and Christine had a great time testing the limits of her driving and Jackie's adrenalin output.

Jackie had taken a three-wheel collapsible scooter with her, one she uses for travelling. It is easy to disassemble and fits in the trunk of a car. Their hotel had a switchback accessibility ramp. After driving over hill and dale and huge moguls all day, Jackie felt she manoeuvred the ramp with supreme skill. Everyone else had a four-inch step to get into the hotel, but Jackie used the ramp. She smiled to herself as she thought, *I guess there are some benefits to being physically challenged.*

On Saturday night, dinner for the jamboree attendees was being served in the resort's restaurant next to the hotel. As usual, Jackie was late and in a rush. She knew better than to rush but didn't always listen to her better judgment. She sailed out of the hotel door and thought she could jump the step. After all, she'd been in a four-wheel-drive jeep all day going over any and every obstacle in nature. This was just a four-inch step.

Christine was right behind her and saw the whole event. It happened in slow motion, she said. Jackie launched herself off the little step, sailed into the air and came gracefully down on her side still sitting in the scooter with the wheels still spinning. Jackie found that if she cocked her head to the side, everything looked perfectly normal. Christine said she was shocked at first, but when Jackie flew into the air like a slow-motion version of Harry Potter on his quidditch stick, she couldn't help but laugh. Christine said that Jackie landed perfectly on the path, just sideways. Apparently, she looked like the character with the tricycle who keeps falling over on the TV show *Laugh In*.

Jackie didn't hurt herself physically; she just wounded her pride. The restaurant had large windows, and everyone had seen Jackie's flying leap. People rushed over, pulled Jackie to her feet and pushed her scooter upright. Jackie dusted herself off, sat back on the scooter and said, "Thank you, I'm okay."

Then she scooted off to the jeep and drove to the town a few miles away for dinner by herself. After that performance she couldn't face Christine's colleagues.

In the end, Jackie decided to do the jeep 101 course herself, in a jeep. She found she could still manage a four-wheel-drive vehicle and do at least some of the elements required to pass the course.

Jackie was awarded the full jeep 101 certificate, which is now framed and hanging on a wall in her home. In the end, she was really proud of herself!

JUST GET ON WITH IT!

The more we study, the more we discover our ignorance

Percy Bysshe Shelley

P am loved being a teacher. Her two siblings were also teachers, as their parents had been before them. You might say teaching was in Pam's blood. But in Pam's case, it was not always clear who was teaching whom, and she liked it this way. In fact, she had set up her own system of "teaching on demand."

Pam started the "Child-Centred Education Program" at her school, which meant the students chose the order and speed in which they completed the curriculum. She and another teacher saw the students through grades two, three and four in this program. Being in the program meant Pam was particularly proud of the ownership her students felt for their own education, even at the tender age of seven. Evidence of their attitude toward learning was especially visible on days when teachers were unexpectedly absent.

In classes taught in the conventional style, the teacher is front and centre directing the students in which topics they should address and how. When the teacher is absent, the lack of authority and direction in the classroom results in very unscholarly forms of noise and bedlam as students celebrate their unaccustomed freedom.

Pam's teaching style was very different. Her students took slips of paper from a "choosing board" in their classroom. Each slip offered the student an assignment or other activity to complete. If they needed help or advice, the students asked the teacher. At times when the teacher was not available, the students knew they had to choose activities they could manage on their own or with another student's help. They learned to manage their time responsibly, as Pam's conventional colleagues could confirm, often somewhat enviously. When Pam wasn't there, her students just got on with their work without her, quietly—as normal. Long before they knew the meaning of the words, her students understood that she was there to facilitate, not to direct, their education.

At thirty, after she had already been teaching for seven years, Pam was diagnosed with multiple sclerosis. Her health concerns, mainly bouts of fatigue, bladder control problems and some numbness and tingling in her hands and feet, were no secret from her colleagues. Given the common assumptions about MS at that time, Pam knew her colleagues expected her physical abilities to deteriorate quickly and that she would soon have to leave teaching. She felt an undercurrent of pity from them which she abhorred.

But these assumptions didn't take into account Pam's application of her child-centred educational philosophy to her own life. When she drew the MS slip, Pam did her own research rather than passively relying on the information her medical doctors gave her; she found them much too pessimistic for her liking. Pam's doctors told her they could not explain the cause of her health challenges and that they had no knowledge of how to cure them. In the present information age, it's easy to think of doing one's own research as normal, but this attitude wasn't normal in the 1960s when Pam decided to take charge of her own health. Doctors were generally considered to have all the answers, and not accepting this was evidence of a character flaw. Pam could identify with James Dean in the movie *Rebel Without a Cause*, except that her cause was her passion for teaching, and her fight was against anything that threatened this work.

Pam decided there had to be something she could do to improve her health—that the problem came from within herself and her life even if no one understood exactly where yet. She took ownership of her project and got on with the job of bringing herself back to good health. She followed every lead through telephone calls, library research and reading mountains of medical papers. She found evidence that her diet was crucial to maintaining health after the onset of MS symptoms. She also read as much research as she could find by a maverick neurologist who was making claims about the beneficial effects of a special diet on MS symptoms. Once Pam was convinced, she followed his advice to the letter, which meant she never ate sweets, pizza or other "empty calories," drank only water or herbal tea, and learned to love liver, broccoli and flax seeds among other healthy foods.

Pam stayed well enough to continue to teach. She never talked about her health at school, and her colleagues never asked her about it. Pam was a slim, regal looking woman who was friendly and quick to smile but very private. She never allowed her worries or special dietary choices to interfere with the work she loved. On days when her fatigue was bad, her years of experience and high level of comfort with her day-to-day activities with the children helped pull her through to better times.

Pam's child-centred education program thrived. She and her teaching partner became known around the province for their innovative work. Her program got unusually good results in a poor urban neighbourhood where it was common for students to fail and have a high rate of absenteeism. The parents of Pam's students often had little education themselves and didn't make school a high priority for their children. But Pam's students developed their own values, and the success and sense of achievement they experienced in school no doubt helped them value education more highly than their parents did.

Pam felt honoured when her program was featured on a national television program. A camera crew came to her classroom and filmed its activities, beaming them live to the program's broadcast centre two thousand miles away. However, she was shocked to learn that the show's on-camera host had a critic of child-centred education in the studio with him. Pam was to present its positive side in a debate that had not been mentioned when she was asked to participate. After the initial shock of realization, she spoke eloquently of how the program helped her students in the crucial tasks of building self-esteem and self-responsibility as well as learning reading, writing, arithmetic and social skills. Pam's passion for her work shone through, and she felt relieved to be given the last word on the subject. The television crew congratulated her on articulating the concepts well and allowing her passion to overshadow the criticism she faced so unexpectedly on live television.

Some time later, the school principal who had supported Pam's program from the start retired. The new principal, Constance, seemed suspicious of Pam's approach and was uncomfortable answering parents' questions about it. In any event, she never promoted it and never asked Pam any questions that might have helped her understand it better. This didn't seem to matter much because the parents who saw their children engaged and happy with their schoolwork supported the program. It was promoted through word of mouth, and the program always had as many students as it could accommodate.

Pam kept her health challenges private from Constance as she did with her other colleagues, but she was sure the new principal would hear gossip about her MS. Although nothing was ever discussed, Pam felt she got more intense scrutiny from the principal in the staffroom than some of the other teachers. However, Pam continued behaving as normally as possible in public, keeping all of her health-promoting activities private.

One day Pam and Constance were walking together along a hallway to meet with the mother of one of Pam's students in the principal's office. For no apparent reason,

Pam tripped and fell down hard. One moment she was talking about her approach to her student's difficulties with reading, the next she was staring at the details of the scuff marks on the waxed floor tiles beneath her face. Pam remembered the fall in the same way she'd heard car drivers talk about the split-second before a collision. Time shifted into slow motion and felt like it almost stopped completely until the disaster ended. Pam's thoughts in that fraction of a second were vivid but leisurely and detached.

How on earth did this happen? Pam wondered as she fell. Then realizing her cheek bone was going to hit the floor, she thought, *I hope this doesn't leave a big bruise or a black eye. If it does I'll have another blot in my copybook. People will think I'm getting beaten up at home. But I'll just have to get up and act normal so Constance has no reason to think of me as sick and incompetent. She has a hard enough time accepting my program. The last thing I need is to give her evidence that I am some kind of weirdo.*

Without acknowledging the fall or the stinging pain in her cheek, Pam immediately picked herself up. She took a few quick steps forward to Constance's side, touched the principal's elbow and carried on walking along the hallway. She continued their conversation about her student with reading difficulties as though nothing had happened.

"You know, Stewart is only eight years old," Pam said. "In a country like Denmark, he would only just be starting school, and structured play would be the main activity. Maybe his mother is expecting too much of him. Or maybe she wants him to make up for a sense of inadequacy she has with her own reading. We can invite her to volunteer in the program, although I know she has a job as a waitress. I'm sure this meeting will be very helpful for all of us."

Before Constance had time to reply, they were at her office door and Stewart's mother was just inside.

Pam never talked about her fall with any of her colleagues. To Pam, the fall was a little frightening, but what she found even more frightening was the thought of not teaching. That evening she made an extra glass of fresh vegetable juice and said an extra prayer. A special homeopathic cream she had ordered from Germany helped keep the bruise on her cheek as small as possible. With a little make-up over it, it was just a shadow on her face, hardly visible unless she looked closely.

Pam carried on teaching until she was fifty-five and eligible for early retirement. She had taught for thirty-two years, twenty-five of them under the shadow of MS. Pam would miss the children and her work with them, but it was time for her to leave. Her health concerns still needed a lot of attention, and her recent marriage gave her another set of priorities.

A year into her retirement, Pam fell again. This fall was similar to the one beside her principal, but this time she couldn't just get up and keep walking. She ended up spending over four months in hospital. She had fractured the top of her right femur into seventeen pieces in a way that required multiple surgeries and steel pins to realign the fractured bone. She was told her slim frame had osteoporosis in almost every bone. Although it was a challenge, with the help of family and friends, Pam managed to continue her healthy diet regime with fresh vegetable juices every day she was in the hospital. Pam's right leg ended up only half an inch shorter than the left, which was much better than her doctors had prepared her to expect.

After her release from hospital, Pam worked every day to build bone mass and strength by doing weight-bearing exercises with rubber tubing. After only one year of dedicated effort, Pam's doctors determined that her bones were strong and free of osteoporosis.

Still a teacher at heart, Pam decided to teach classes on the techniques and benefits of exercising with rubber tubing. She got a great deal of interest from other seniors in the village to which she moved after retiring. Along with this commitment, Pam often joined her husband on his sailboat helping him give the "learn to sail" charters that paid the boat's expenses. She also found time to write a book about her experience with child-centred education and self-publish and promote her father's war memoirs.

Pam kept going back to her personal life "choosing board" for new challenges whenever she achieved a goal she set for herself. Her most recent accomplishment was walking two miles along the beach without her cane. Her "choosing board" still has many slips on it, with projects that will always keep her learning and fully engaged in life. Pam makes sure of that. Life is good, she will tell you with a smile if you ask. And then she just gets on with it!

THE SOLSTICE PARTY

To everything there is a season, and a time to every purpose under the heavens.

Ecclesiastes 3:1-8

I grew up on a mixed farm in a conservative Mennonite settlement in the middle of the Canadian prairie. As a teenager I thought my farm life was medieval even though I knew I lived in the so-called modern world. As an adult, I value my appreciation of the land and the turning of the seasons that just came naturally with my upbringing.

Our farm had several large garden plots that we planted with potatoes every year. In spring, I had to help cut the seed potatoes into pieces that each had an "eye" that would grow into the new plant. Then my father and brothers dug the holes into which my sister, my mother and I planted the potato pieces. We took care to have the potato eye facing upward and press it into the hole which the men then refilled with soil. My mother preferred red potatoes while my father was partial to white ones, so we always planted some of each variety.

As summer progressed, the potato plant tops grew tall and bushy. First we weeded the long rows; then as the growing season progressed the plants were "hilled." For hilling we heaped soil around the base of each plant so the potatoes growing just beneath the surface stayed well-covered. In some years, infestations of what we called "potato bugs" had to be plucked off the plant leaves. As the youngest children not yet trusted with operating heavy machinery, these jobs were assigned to me and my older sister.

Potato field jobs were something I suffered through. I always let the sun get high overhead before I started, and so I ended up working when it was unpleasantly hot. I never followed my sister's good example of getting up early enough to hoe or hill the rows for which I was responsible before the heat built up.

In autumn the men dug the potatoes out of the soil with forks, and the women collected them in buckets and sacks. The potatoes were stored in the root cellar of our house through the winter. Although we ate potatoes every day, my mother always made sure there were enough left for another season of planting. Then the cycle started all over again.

If I close my eyes even now, the damp, earthy smell of the potatoes in the root cellar comes flooding back; its memory still visceral. It was my favourite smell as a child, and no other memory of my farm life is as evocative as this one.

I also had to help my mother with her summer work of making pickles and sauerkraut, and picking and preserving fruit by freezing or canning it. We grew raspberries—my favourites—strawberries, gooseberries and black currants, and we drove to the riverbanks to pick wild blueberries.

Every autumn we killed animals to have meat through the winter, freezing the best cuts and making smoked sausages from the scraps. As a child, I thought oxtail was the most exotic delicacy as we only had it once a year. Animal fat was rendered into lard and "cracklings" to eat on toast made with flour ground from wheat grown in our own fields.

Autumn was always the most exciting season for me. Harvesting required long hours of hard work, and my parents were too busy to enforce the usual controls in my life. Pursuing forbidden freedoms was my highest early teenage priority, and during the harvest I'd be admonished to get my work done before I went off with my friends to play softball or hang out drinking Coke in the village café.

Although my family moved off the farm when I was sixteen, my father planted a garden every year until he was ninety six. He only stopped because his knees became too painful for him to take care of it. One of the last years he planted potatoes he dug them out in July. I asked why he did this so early. He told me he had seen a mould on the plant tops which was a sign that the potatoes would not taste good if they stayed in the soil until maturity. He judged it best to have small but tasty potatoes early.

As a child, I was more than a little embarrassed by what I considered my parents' old-fashioned way of life, but as an adult I marvel at the range of knowledge they needed to survive and thrive as farmers. I buy my potatoes and other food in a supermarket now, but the increasingly rare knowledge of how to grow it and where it comes from strikes me as important. I asked my father questions about how he knew what we had to do to live off the land. I think he found my rather sociological approach a little strange.

"We just knew," was his matter-of-fact reply to most of my questions.

When I insisted on more details, he said, "We did what our parents taught us, and we learned from our mistakes or ones our neighbours made. We judged how warm and moist the soil was to decide when to plant. We didn't change things without good reasons, and we always watched the sky, the birds and wild animals."

I felt there was much more to my father's knowledge and resolved to tape record some of his stories the next time I saw him.

Twenty years after I left my family's prairie farm, I lived a thousand miles away by the sea. Here I developed health problems which my doctors labelled multiple sclerosis. I learned that this chronic illness occurs at higher levels in my home province than elsewhere in the country, and that there was a "hot spot" of MS not far away from where I grew up. Almost half the population of a village of four hundred have this illness. Many of them probably grew up as I did, eating a diet made up almost entirely of homegrown foods. Perhaps there were deficiencies in our soil that predisposed me to MS, but whether that is the case or not, growing up on the land rooted me in nature in ways I've only valued as I grow older.

When I first moved to the coast, I stayed fit by walking from my home through a forest park to an ocean beach and back. If my time was short, I could complete this walk in an hour. But it was one of those pleasures that always expanded to fit the time available, and I could easily fill the better part of an afternoon or evening. On the longest day of the year, I made sure I was at the beach to watch the sun go down.

Advancing disability soon meant I had to use a scooter to get around outside my house, but I was grateful I could continue visiting my favourite beach. I just watched the sun set on the summer solstice from the seat of my scooter instead of from a driftwood log on the sand.

To be able to appreciate nature all year round in all kinds of weather, I created a special garden visible through my front windows. I celebrated its completion with a party for my friends on the summer solstice. As background for this occasion, I read a book on solstice celebrations around the world. I was surprised to learn that the Egyptian pyramids and Stonehenge were originally built as "calendars" to help track the changing of the seasons. Apparently, well-known landmarks from every ancient culture on every continent were specially designed to allow the priests and priestesses to determine exactly when the solstice and equinox occurred. I also read that the year is considered masculine while the hours of sunlight are contracting and feminine while the hours of sunlight are expanding. So my garden party marked the start of the masculine half of the year.

I decided I'd also celebrate the winter solstice to mark the start of the feminine half of the year. I invited just a few friends, none of whom knew one another, to share the occasion. The main event would be an outdoor fire in which we would symbolically burn what we didn't want to carry forward into a new year. The fire could also remind us that the summer sunlight would return. The ancient Celts apparently lit fire to tree bough "wheels" which they rolled down hills in a ritual invitation to the sun to bring its light and warmth back to their lands. My winter solstice party would resonate with these ancient traditions.

For party refreshments, my first plan was to keep it very simple and serve raw vegetables, rice crackers and sparkling apple juice. This was what I could eat and all I could manage to prepare on my own. Michael had a nasty flu virus, and I didn't want to ask for his help. However, he thought I needed to serve more interesting food and went out shopping for me. He came home with wine, smoked salmon and a variety of cheeses, crackers and fruit. He laid the food out on our most festive plates and brought out our best glasses.

On the winter solstice, we sat talking, eating and laughing as my friends are all artists along with their other work, family and community roles. Monika is a writer as I am. Marsha is a lithographer, Alma a singer, and Helen a dancer, actor and painter.

At dusk, when the food was mostly gone, we put on our coats and went outside. Michael had laid a large piece of metal on the deck for the fire. I started the ritual by placing a dried out Christmas wreath made of cedar boughs and pine cones on the metal and lighting it. I said that the wreath symbolized my fear. By eliminating fear, I was making space for the health and other good things I wanted to come into my life.

Each of my friends put something in the fire. Marsha burned a dusting sock as she hates housework and wants less of it. Monika also burned fear, especially of poverty, symbolized by words written on a piece of paper. Later that year, she told me the ritual burning had created powerful magic, as she had contracted more well-paid writing projects than usual. Alma burned a piece of paper with words she said symbolized all the "past crap" she didn't want in her future. These words made Helen smile and echo the sentiment of burning unwanted "past crap" through her offering to the fire.

Each one of us around the fire on that winter solstice ritually released the burdens and fears of the old year. We invited divine help to open ourselves and realize our hearts' deepest desires, and each of us made real progress toward them in the new year.

The sun brought another summer of glorious warmth and natural bounty back, of course. I'm grateful I no longer have to weed or hill in the fields to enjoy all the organic potatoes I want. Nature's bounty is still available to me, although it feels less immediate in my modern adult life than it did working on the farm in my childhood.

I still need my wheelchair, but my efforts to restore my health are bearing fruit. I accept that my desire for wellness will manifest in God's time, which moves with the slow, stately pace of the seasons. But I feel more at peace with every passing day. Whatever my future holds, I'll meet it without fear and with that most precious of gifts, my friends.

WATER, FREEDOM AND LOVE

Healing is the gradual awakening to the perfection
of your life.

Martin Lass

L inley loved swimming and always felt free when
she was in the water. Lin, as she was known to her
friends, lived close to an ocean beach and a large
seawater pool. When the summer heat got too high for
comfort, she kept cool in the seawater pool. The grassy
verge by the beach was a great place to meet people or
just watch them. As the seasons advanced to winter and
the sun spent less time warming her northern home, Lin
watched the water's moods through her window, staying
close to the warm glow of her fireplace. On New Year's
Day, she always watched the polar bear swim. Even from
a distance, many of the people preparing to enter the
frigid seawater looked more than a little hung-over to Lin.
*No doubt they're hoping for a quick cure to a New Year's Eve of
extreme partying*, Lin thought as she watched and shivered
under her winter sweaters. *But they'll probably just get a cold or
the flu. The water looks close to freezing, even if it is salty.*

She recalled news reports about the Swedes being the healthiest people in the world. They apparently advocated the benefits of cold water swimming followed by the heat of a sauna. Lin decided that even if they had a point, she'd look for other ways to restore her health—ways that emphasized the sauna. Lin preferred tropical waters for swimming in winter. Locally, she only went into the sea after a low tide when the sun-warmed sands heated the water as it flowed in over them. But even that pleasure was a distant memory.

Twenty-one years before, Lin's doctors had told her she had multiple sclerosis. She gradually lost more and more control in her limbs over those years, but she never lost her spirit of adventure. People usually responded with admiration to what they typically described as her brave resolve to live "normally" when they heard or read about her latest travel adventures. Lin was a travel writer who wrote articles offering "how to" information to others with disabilities. This work also helped generate travel perks and discounts for her.

One hot summer day after she'd been in the pool, Lin sat in her wheelchair on the grassy verge by the beach watching the tide come in. The sight generated a powerful ache in her body to be in the ocean, to feel the pull of the tide. It was an ache too strong for her to ignore. She looked around and saw the well-muscled man she had watched take a cooling dip just a few minutes earlier. Now he was moving his beach towel to face the sun just a short distance away. Lin could see drops of water still glistening in his chest hair. She rolled over and smiled down at him, watching his friendly brown eyes watch her approach.

"Is the water as perfect as it looks?" Lin asked.

She could feel her own longing to be in the sea again in every fibre of her being.

Browneyes' smile and nod gave his response.

Encouraged, Lin smiled back and observed, "Your muscles look like you work out; have I seen you at our local gym?"

"No," Browneyes said. "Not in a gym. I'm a logger. But right now I'm happy to just be leaning my arms on a driftwood log and watching the tide come in."

Lin smiled her best impish smile and looked down her turned up nose at Browneyes as she said, "Well, you've got the muscles of a bodybuilder, but I guess your chainsaw gives you a workout *and* you'd get paid for it."

Browneyes smiled back at Lin's cleavage, shown to full advantage in her bikini top.

"You probably do some weightlifting yourself, getting in and out of that wheelchair. Your triceps are very well-developed for a woman."

Lin knew she had lucked out. Browneyes was showing promise as a man who was not afraid of her disability. She kept the light-hearted banter going for a while and then cut to the chase.

"I'd love to get in the water myself, but this chair's motor would just short out even if I could get it to take me across the sand. Any chance of a lift into the tide waters?"

Browneyes smiled back at Lin, "You're asking me to put my arms around you and carry you into the sea? You're my kind of woman! Let's go!"

Browneyes carried Lin to the water's edge and gently set her down on the sandy bottom. Lin sighed with pleasure and relief as she splashed her face with the cooling water. Her companion watched and then decided to help with vigorous splashing that soaked both of them. Lin turned her face to the sun and licked the salty brine from her lips. The two of them giggled like children as they sat on the sand and played in the water.

The tide rolled in quickly, and it was waist-high to Lin and Browneyes before long. Well-cooled and still smiling, Browneyes held out his hand to Lin and said, "I guess I should know your name before I carry you back to your chair. I'm Rob Dundas."

Lin introduced herself and then draped her body over Rob's back for the journey out of the sea. Rob set Lin down on his log while he covered her wheelchair seat with his towel. Then he picked her up again and gently placed her wet body on her wheelchair.

Before they parted that afternoon, Rob asked Lin for her phone number. Over the next few months, they went out whenever Rob had some time out of "the bush," as he called his logging camp home. Their relaxed appreciation of each other's company felt good to Lin, although one thing about Rob puzzled her. Even though he was happy to hear about her travel adventures, Rob was curiously silent about his own. Lin found out why when she invited him to join her on a trip to Costa Rica. His pained response answered all her speculations.

"I can't leave Canada. I have a criminal drug conviction on my record. Even if Costa Rica would let me in, the United States won't let me transit. I'd love to come with you, but I can't."

Lin asked Rob some questions about this revelation of his past. He said he was helping a friend who cultivated marijuana in a forest clearing when they were both caught and later convicted. When he finished telling Lin his story, Rob sighed and said, "Life will never be simple again. I've often wished I'd made friends with the guys who hunt morel mushrooms in their time off. They make as much money as the pot growers, and they can travel wherever they like. They're revered in Japan. But still, this is the way it is for me. I'll have to experience your adventures second hand."

Some weeks after this conversation, Lin left for Costa Rica with another friend. The highlight of the trip came at Playa Blanca when a guide carried Lin to the beach to watch giant tortoises scoop nests and lay their eggs in the warm sand. She absorbed every detail she saw and felt of the turtles' raw instinct for propagation. She knew it was something that had to be experienced—not even the best *National Geographic* cameraman could capture the intensity of the moment on film. She felt honoured by the turtles' tolerance of her presence. It was an experience she knew she'd never forget.

This trip got Lin thinking about her own instincts and desires for a mate to share not only the special moments, but also the mundane details of everyday life. She enjoyed Rob's company but knew she needed more than they had together. Perhaps he felt it, too, because Rob never did call again.

After some careful wording and a lot of good-humoured ribbing from her friends, Lin placed an ad describing her needs and wants from a man in a weekly newspaper she enjoyed. Although she never held much hope, Lin got more response than she'd ever expected. After a few months of dating men who turned out to be unsuitable for one reason or another, she met Liam. He shared her love of travel and could match her passion for adventurous travel. Liam was also very comfortable with Lin's disability. He appeared to know himself well and felt Lin could meet his own need to be needed and appreciated for even the smallest things in life.

A few months after they met, Lin decided it was time to ask Liam if he thought he'd be comfortable sharing her apartment. Liam accepted the invitation and together they discovered they shared a long-held dream of driving the Alaska Highway. Liam started looking for a van to make travelling with Lin easier. While Lin and Liam were debating whether to wait for the right van to be advertised or to find one they could customize to their needs, Lin got an offer to write an article about disabled travel on the big island of Hawaii. There was no debate about whether they would go.

Although they were staying in another Kona Coast Hotel, Lin contacted the one she knew had a pool lift for the disabled the day after they arrived. She spoke with a man called Paul who had a broad Texan accent.

"Don't you worry your head, ma'am. We'll git you in our pool," he promised.

Paul was as good as his word and invited Lin and Liam to come swimming any time they wanted no matter where they were staying. In one of their conversations, Paul asked Lin if she had ever been snorkelling.

"Years ago when I was a lot more able than I am now," Lin said wistfully. "I really enjoyed it, but I don't think I'm up to it now."

Paul was not a man to be easily dissuaded. He was convinced that with a little planning, practice and help, Lin could snorkel in the ocean again. This encouragement was all it took for Lin to invest six dollars in the purchase of a mask and snorkel. She spent the next three days in the pool soaking up Paul's and Liam's help and encouragement. Lin's confidence grew quickly, and Paul soon pronounced her ready for a sea trial.

Instead of being carried to the water's edge, Lin rode in style across the soft sand in the hotel's beach wheelchair with its fat, bouncy tires. Paul and Liam lifted Lin into the water and got her mask and snorkel properly adjusted. They each took one of Lin's hands and guided her for over an hour in the warm tropical sea. They swam beyond the protective rocks close to the shore and out over a nearby coral reef. Lin felt pure joy and elation just being in the buoyant salty sea again. The colourful fish darting off as the threesome passed made seeing the reef through her mask even more exotic.

Lin reflected as she floated over the reef, *Fish move like this by instinct, and today I'm one with them. My snorkel lets me breathe like a fish. In the water I'm free again!* Before this thought was complete, a large green sea turtle swam by so close that Lin could have touched its hard, mottled shell. Lin imagined she saw a quizzical look in the turtle's eyes as it passed her, and she couldn't help wondering if she had been present for its birth in Costa Rica. Lin's heart felt full with the thrill of discovery again! As the turtle swam out of sight, she remembered they are considered symbols of protection and longevity in some cultures. She smiled below her snorkel, feeling protected by her companions—and as though this moment was all the time that was.

Lin found it very easy to "just be" with Liam's caring acceptance in her life. Paul's attitude, her snorkel and the beach wheelchair gave her a first Hawaiian holiday with Liam that she'd never forget. Lin's life of travel adventures so far had given her both joy and a living. Now she had a partner to share each new travel discovery and pleasure as well as stress.

Lin felt deeply that if Liam could accept and love her just as she was, it lit a path for her to accept and love herself just as she was. She could live fully in the present moment. Her writing and photo albums told the stories of her past. The future would unfold as a new adventure every day. She felt complete and at peace!

WOW!!

When Grandmothers take us for walks, they slow down past things like pretty leaves and caterpillars. They talk to us about why flowers are different colours, and why we shouldn't step on cracks. They don't say, "Hurry up." Grandmothers answer questions like "Why isn't God married?" and "How come dogs chase cats?" When they read to us, they don't skip. They don't mind if we ask for the same story over and over again. They know that snack-time always comes before bedtime, and kiss us even when we've been bad.

Anonymous

V iolet loved being a grandmother. She enjoyed the peace of feeling that all her child-rearing mistakes were behind her, and that her time with Christopher, her grandson, came without downsides like laundry or tantrums. And Christopher returned her love unconditionally.

His mannerisms always made Violet laugh no matter how fatigued she felt. Even just toddling across the room in a diaper, he'd look back over his shoulder, smiling mischievously and checking to make sure Violet was watching.

Christopher called Violet "Nanna." This name was a holdover from the earliest months of his life when forming any sound was pure imitation. Christopher started speaking two- or three-word sentences at ten months old. Everyone remarked on the clarity of his speech at this young age, saying he'd grow up to be an actor, a politician or some other occupation where he'd use this gift.

Now Christopher was two and starting to assert himself, establishing his independence in the warmth and safety of the love that surrounded him. Violet delighted in watching him grow and change. She felt particularly blessed to have Christopher and his parents—her daughter, Leigh, and son-in-law, Mark—living just a few blocks away from her. Especially when she developed a mild intermittent tremor on top of her other neurological dysfunctions.

Leigh and Mark took Violet grocery shopping every week or to any appointments she had. Every Sunday they took her to mass at her favourite church, the old cathedral downtown, which was a half-hour drive from the suburb where they lived. Violet wished she could reciprocate in some way, but Leigh and Mark always reassured her that helping her was no trouble.

"There's no cause for your worry," Leigh told her repeatedly. "Your needs fit in with ours and don't take any extra effort on our part. We love the old cathedral downtown just as much as you do. All of us were baptized there, and we got married there, so it's part of our lives too. And we just add your shopping into the lists of what we have to do for ourselves."

Still, Violet always tried to be as independent as possible, minimizing her calls on Leigh's and Mark's time.

Christopher seemed to think it was very special to have a Nanna who picked up her cup with both hands just like he did. And when Violet's tremors caused her head to shake, Christopher tried to imitate the motion.

"Nanna, do more," he'd say with a smile that told Violet he thought this was a very special and entertaining talent.

Then Violet developed a new movement problem. Her doctor called it Sydenham's chorea, but Violet preferred the name she found for it on the internet: St. Vitus' Dance. She found this label for the movements that unexpectedly transported her to another dimension more poetic, a better match for her experience of the problem than its prosaic medical name.

However, the internet description of the choreic movements of St. Vitus' Dance didn't quite agree with Violet's experience of them. She felt them as fluid and dreamlike, both voluntary and involuntary at the same time. The medical description of the Dance was that it consisted of movements that were rapid and irregular, uncontrollable and jerky. Violet agreed that they involved her trunk, arms and legs, although she couldn't be sure of any face and neck involvement in her case since she had never seen her St. Vitus movements in a mirror. So far, Violet had only experienced three episodes of the Dance.

On a lovely autumn Monday, Leigh decided to take Christopher to the park to feed the ducks. He loved throwing the grain into the water off the little bridge over a narrowing of the pond. He'd gleefully call to the birds as they came from all shores to gobble up the bounty. If one of the ducks chased off others in an attempt to scoop up more food for itself, he could not hide his indignance.

"Share!" he'd command from his crouching position watching from between the railing boards of the bridge. "Mommy say share!"

When the pond's resident turtles showed their red-patched heads from beneath the surface, Christopher became transfixed. He had a lot of questions about the lives of ducks and turtles. Did they like one another? Where did they sleep at night?

This particular Monday, Violet felt she'd be better off at home resting. However, with the sun shining after several days of rain, she decided to go along when Leigh and Christopher stopped by to ask if she wanted to join them in a trip to the park just a few blocks away. Violet put on her sweater, and the three of them walked in the crisp, sunny air with Christopher setting the pace, his stroller carrying the grain for the birds and turtles. Christopher chattered happily to himself, hopping over cracks in the sidewalk and talking to the spiders and ants that shared their route.

Twenty minutes later, Christopher threw the grain into the water of the pond with gusto, calling to the ducks and admonishing them to "Share nicely." The turtles must have been happy the sun was shining, too, because three of them made an appearance after the ducks' commotion settled down. Christopher whispered to Violet about their presence, and gave her what was left of the bag of grain.

"Feed turtles, Nanna. You feel better," he said.

Violet smiled as she scattered handfuls of grain on the water. *He must be psychic,* she thought. She had not said anything about feeling under the weather, but Christopher sensed her malaise.

With the grain gone, the ducks swam away to a grassy section of the pond, and the turtles sank silently out of sight under the murky water. The foursome stepped back on the path toward home while Christopher happily recapped the visit. They had only walked about forty feet when Violet realized something was going to happen. She felt the movement take over her body like an alien, but friendly, visitation. It seemed as though time stopped while St. Vitus moved her like a graceful, ballet-dancing puppet on strings. She felt her trunk lean forward and her arms extend outward, palms toward the sky. She made a full pirouette. Her eyes took in the patterns in the gravel around the toes of her left foot. Then her weight shifted to the right foot. Her eyes observed the blue sky with its scattering of clouds high above the treetops as she continued to circle. Violet felt as though her fingers were trailing through the cool mists of the clouds, as though she had ascended to a place closer to God. Then the movement stopped as unexpectedly as it began, and her old realities came back like an old black-and-white movie scene being overwritten with the action and colour of a modern one.

As in her previous episodes of the Dance, Violet's steps were fluid, outside of time. She felt as though her brain was in exquisite control of her movements and balance. As her sense of time and motion returned to normal, Violet found herself standing upright with Leigh behind her. Christopher was utterly entranced, as though his world had been touched by magic. His face told of wonderment, of awe and amazement at what he had witnessed.

"Wow!!" Christopher exclaimed.

That said it all.

Leigh smiled through a look of concern. She gently took Violet's arm and asked if she wanted to sit down.

"No," Violet said. "I'll lie down when I get home."

Violet's fourth episode of this strange new disorder was completely overshadowed by Christopher's smile and delight. His two-year-old version of speechlessness moved her heart. Had he been able to say more, Violet was sure Christopher would have declared proudly to all the world, "Look what my Nanna can do! She's special!"

The three of them walked slowly through the park and then along the sidewalk to Violet's house. Christopher held Violet's hand. She knew she would always remember this day and the innocence and wonder of a child's view of life. *To some*, she thought, *St. Vitus might be a thief. But to Christopher, it brings magic into the world. It's all a question of how you look at things, and I'm with Christopher. After all, he's named after the patron saint of travellers. My travel is a little different to what I'd expected for my golden years, but whatever happens, the look on Christopher's face today has given me a memory I value beyond anything that's usually thought of as worldly treasure.*

DOPPLER IN THE CAR WASH

The truth is a matter of perception.

William Ginsburg

Diane smiled as she moved the gearshift of her car from neutral to drive and pulled away from the curb outside Joe's Diner. She'd just spent a very pleasant three hours with friends eating a lunch that someone else had cooked. Now another nameless person who didn't need to be reminded several times, as her children did, was washing the dirty dishes. Much as she'd enjoyed her lunch out, Diane also appreciated being able to cook and do her own housework again. Driving her new car felt more like the icing on the chocolate cake she'd ordered for dessert.

Diane was a driver with a difference. This simple task was not one she'd ever take for granted again. She had spent twenty-one years being driven by others. The memory of her first car trip was still vivid. The van that was her normal mode of transport was being serviced, and her son had just passed his driver's license test. He'd been entrusted with the family car because Diane needed to get to an appointment. She was one of five passengers, and the only adult. Diane was just happy to have a ride and was actually enjoying being jammed in between two husky sixteen year olds while Guns and Roses blared through the speakers and out the open windows. Although the music was not to her taste, the alternative was staying home and rescheduling her treatment. In the van, she travelled in the back in her wheelchair. She enjoyed her view through the car windows, and if her son was driving her where she wanted to go, she was happy to let him choose the music.

After that first car trip, it took another sixteen years and thousands of hours of hard work before Diane regained her ability to walk. Later, she passed the road test for her driver's license and added another milestone in the recovery of her independence. This time the privilege meant a lot more to her than it had when she was sixteen. The van that had transported Diane in her wheelchair remained her vehicle now that she could drive herself. It was big and difficult to manoeuvre, but she cherished the independence it gave her.

Diane lived in a city that endured cold and snowy winters, which meant a lot of salt was used to keep the roads free of ice. She'd always made sure her van was washed regularly to prevent rusting. Now that she could drive again, Diane decided she would tackle the job rather than try to get her sons to do it. She felt that if she was able enough to drive the van, she should be able to wash it. She'd applied this logic to her children many times.

The only car wash that was high enough for her van had four washing bays under one roof. Diane drove into the only empty space and loaded the coin tray with quarters. She pulled the trigger on the sprayer hose and started washing the salt spray from the bottom of her van. All went well until she tried to wash the top of the van. Diane is not quite five feet, three inches tall, and her van was at least two feet higher than her head. The sprayer didn't bend enough to reach the top of the van properly. Diane tried valiantly, spraying as high as she could reach. She knew the top of her van was safe from the road salt, but she liked to be thorough.

While she was still trying to wash the top of her van, a man holding a child approached her from another bay.

"I've been washing my car in the next bay," he said with a smile. "I see you're struggling to wash the top of your van. Maybe I can help."

"I'd be grateful," Diane replied. Then she saw how wet the man and his child were. "Did I do that?" she asked pointing to their sodden clothes.

"Well, yes, we've been getting showered along with your van. It helps if you're a little taller or you use one of the stools they keep along the side," he said, pointing to a small metal stepladder near the wall.

Seeing Diane's woeful face, he quickly repeated his offer of help.

"We'll make it a trade. I'll wash the top of your van if you watch my son."

Diane thankfully took her helper's child, and together they watched him make short work of cleaning her van's roof from the top of a stepladder.

This incident showed Diane she still had a lot to learn to fit in with the changes that had happened while she was sick. Deciding it was time to put the past behind her, Diane bought a smaller vehicle, a new compact car. It was a treat to drive, especially since her vehicle no longer reminded her of the years she'd spent in a wheelchair.

After a few weeks of driving her new car over salty roads, Diane decided it was time to clean it. Having heard the story of child-minding while someone else washed the top of her van, Diane's friends told her about the new automatic car washes with machines that did everything while the driver just sat behind the wheel. They described it laughingly as analogous to driving through an intense soap storm.

Feeling too cold and tired to go to the manual car wash she knew, Diane decided it was time to try one of the new automatic places. She had discovered one at a gas station not far from her daughter's school, so she pulled up to the concession booth and asked the attendant on duty how the car wash worked. The attendant looked about sixteen and was much more interested in his comic book than in answering Diane's questions. He barely raised his eyes as he pointed and said, "You put your credit card in the machine and just follow directions."

Diane drove to the automatic pay station. She saw a neon screen directing her to put her credit card in the slot. She fumbled through her purse and dug the card out of her wallet. She rolled her window open and reached out with her credit card. There was about a twelve-inch gap between the card and its designated slot even though Diane's car was as close as she'd been able to get to the pay box. She realized she'd have to unbuckle her seat belt in order to reach it. She pushed the release button and immediately the warning bell started dinging. She reached out to enter her credit card.

The end of her credit card grazed the pay slot but didn't catch. Instead, it dropped to the ground between the cement curb on which the pay station stood and her car. Her seat belt warning bell was still dinging. Diane opened her door to reach down to pick it up. The door opened twelve inches before hitting the pay stand with a metallic crunch. The space was just enough for Diane's arm to reach down and retrieve her card. She left the door open hoping this would allow her the extra space she needed to reach the pay slot.

Diane stretched her arm as far as she could, thinking next time she'd leave enough space to be able to get out of the car and face the pay slot head on. Her heart sank as her credit card fell again. Maybe she wasn't concentrating, maybe she needed new glasses, maybe the world should be run by people instead of machines—all these thoughts ran through her mind as she reached down to pick up her credit card again. Her head was starting to ache. Unwilling to face a third attempt at the pay slot through the car window, Diane backed up and repositioned the car so she could open the car door and get out to stand face to face with the pay slot. *Hurray*! she thought as she finally successfully entered her credit card.

A voice boomed out something about a wax. Diane jumped. She wasn't expecting to be spoken to after her encounter with the teenage attendant and the ordeals entering her credit card.

"I just want a wash," she said in a small voice.

The deep voice boomed out again, "Carnuba wax helps your car look new. Just two dollars extra."

Diane finally convinced the machine that all she wanted was a basic wash. The deep voice confirmed her choice and thanked her. Diane climbed back into the driver's seat and tucked her credit card back into her wallet.

The neon sign ahead advised her to start her engine and pull ahead. Diane followed the directions, feeling her tires driving over a hump. The sign then advised Diane to shift into neutral, which she did. Next the sign asked Diane to wait. She felt tired and gratefully closed her eyes.

A few seconds later, she felt herself start to move. She was sure she had shifted into neutral, and she opened her eyes to check. She had, but there was no doubt about it, she was moving forward. *How is this happening?* she wondered. She put her foot on the brake. No response. *I'm sure these brakes were checked before I bought the car. Why aren't they working now?* Her right foot was still numb, but she was sure she should have stopped by now. She jammed her foot harder onto the brake. She was pressing so hard that she was sliding forward, but she couldn't stop the car from moving. Her knuckles were white on the steering wheel. There was some kind of carpet cut into strips swooshing toward her. It hit her windshield and kept moving over the top of her car.

At least it won't do any damage. She was sure she should have stopped, but it still felt like she was moving. *This is too surreal*, she thought. Her foot was still jammed on the brake. Then she felt something wet on her face. *The carpet strips are coming after me!* Soapy water was dripping down the inside of her window. *I must not have closed it after the credit card debacle*, she thought.

Her foot was still glued to the brake, still trying to stop the car. A big sploosh of soapy water hit her face, causing her to close her eyes. She opened them again when she felt hot air blowing on her face. *How did they know I was wet?* she wondered. *That was nice of them.*

Then she saw a sign that said: "Thanks and have a nice day. Come again."

She was feeling thankful for the hot air, but she'd had a shower that morning. The day was a nice day until the car wash. "Come again"? She didn't think so. But she could see daylight ahead of her. The ordeal was almost over.

Diane realized she could take her foot off the brake and that things were unfolding as they should. She was out of the tunnel, dripping wet inside and out. She couldn't tell how much moisture had come from the sweat of her stress and how much had come from the car wash. As her car inched toward the end, Diane realized she'd have to get her car out of the cavern she was in. If she hadn't been able to stop though, she wondered what would happen when she tried to drive forward.

This thought was still in the back of her wet and foggy brain as she saw the sun through the opening of the car wash exit. She looked through her steamed up glasses at her gearshift wondering what she would tell her husband about the strange brake functions of this new car.

The car was in neutral. That's when the brain fog started to lift.

She had not been driving. She must have been on some kind of belt that was controlling her movement through the car wash. Her first response was a huge sense of relief. Then an equally huge sense of embarrassment followed immediately. *How could she not have remembered the tricks one's eyes can play with opposite motions?* she wondered. Science had been one of her strong subjects at school. It was called the Doppler effect.

After she drove to the nearest parking bay, Diane got out of the car to let the cold air clear her head. Her wet clothes helped, and she got a tissue from her purse to dry her glasses. She laughed out loud, got back in the car and drove home. She told her family the adventure she'd had in the car wash over the dinner table. They all laughed out loud.

9 780228 854487